65

ANIMAL HORMONES

Biological Sciences

Editor
PROFESSOR H. MUNRO FOX
M.A., F.R.S.
*Emeritus Professor of Zoology
in the University of London*

Animal Hormones

J. LEE

*Reader in Physiology, University of London
at Charing Cross Hospital Medical School*

and

F. G. W. KNOWLES

*Reader in Comparative Endocrinology in the Department of Anatomy
University of Birmingham*

HUTCHINSON UNIVERSITY LIBRARY
LONDON

HUTCHINSON & CO (*Publishers*) LTD
178–202 Great Portland Street, London, W1

London Melbourne Sydney
Auckland Bombay Toronto
Johannesburg New York

First published 1965

*This book has been set in Times New Roman, printed
in Great Britain on Smooth Wove paper by The Anchor
Press, Ltd., and bound by Wm. Brendon & Son Ltd.,
both of Tiptree, Essex.*

To our parents

Contents

Preface

This book deals with the hormones of animals, and is intended to guide the reader rather than to provide him with a comprehensive account; for this the reader should refer to the books given in the references. [1-7]

The study of hormones in vertebrates has been developed along two major pathways: by the clinician, who found that in man certain tissues when diseased produced specific effects, and by the discovery by physiologists of chemical messengers secreted into the blood stream. In the vertebrates ablation and replacement procedures are relatively easy to carry out; information from the clinical field has also been very helpful in guiding the experimenter along the correct channels.

The approach to the study of invertebrate endocrinology was different. The development of the subject and the nature of the inherent problems necessitated the use of extracts from tissues believed to be endocrine glands. If these extracts had a specific action it was taken as evidence that they were derived from endocrine glands. It is, however, necessary to establish the specificity of the action and the purity of the extract in the invertebrates, as in the vertebrates. In the section on the invertebrates this aspect is considered in some detail.

The presentation of the chapters on the endocrine glands departs from the usual procedure; in this book the common practice has been to consider their role separately in each class of the Vertebrata. The only real exception is the neurohypophysis, which has not been considered under separate headings. This approach enables the reader to find specific information more easily, but unfortunately it does result in some repetition. On the other hand, this may be of benefit to the student acquiring new information when some re-emphasis may be justified. While the adenohypophysis and the gonads are not considered under separate headings, such as histology, active principles, control and function, in each group of animals, the endocrine glands, thyroid, parathyroids, adrenals, and the islets of Langerhans are discussed thus in order to achieve an easier presentation. As knowledge of the part played by these glands in the foetus is uncertain, only brief reference is made to them and this may appear only in the summaries.

At the time this work was commenced, there was no standard textbook of comparative endocrinology. The students' task has now been made much simpler by the appearance of such books.

We should like to thank Drs J. F. D. Frazer, Angus d'A. Bellairs, J. J. Jones and K. M. Backhouse for their help in the preparation of the manuscript.

I

Introduction

THE word 'hormone' was introduced by Starling (1905)[59] with reference to secretin, a chemical messenger secreted by the duodenal mucosa, which stimulates the digestive secretion of the pancreas. The derivation of hormone was from the Greek ὁρμάω (I excite), but later it became clear that the action of some hormones was to inhibit and not to excite activity. In 1914 Starling[60] defined a hormone as 'any substance normally produced in the cells of some part of the body and carried by the blood stream to distant parts which it affects for the good of the body as a whole'. Organisms, however, which are devoid of a vascular system would, by definition, possess no hormones.

Huxley (1935)[38] suggested the use of the word 'activator', which was defined as a chemical substance produced by the organism to exert a specific effect on correlation or differentiation. He classified these as local and distance activators which were then subdivided as shown in the following table. Circulating activators are interchangeable with hormones as defined previously. The biologist may prefer Huxley's interpretation, but the human physiologist has accepted the original definition, with certain amendments. A convenient definition of a hormone for the human physiologist is, an organic chemical substance secreted into the blood stream by a tissue, which is usually a gland; this substance modifies the activity of other cells, or tissues, in a specific manner.

The term 'local hormone' was introduced to define a chemical substance released locally to produce a specific effect without entering the general circulation. The word 'hormone' has been misused in this phrase and it would have been preferable to refer to local regulators. Despite its unfortunate origin, the term 'local hormone' has been widely accepted[15] and is used in this book.

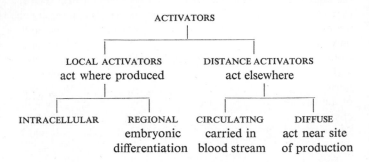

An endocrine gland is one which has no duct (hence sometimes referred to as a ductless gland) and secretes a hormone, or hormones. Thus, to establish that a tissue is an endocrine gland, it is essential to demonstrate that it secretes a hormone into the blood. This could be shown by direct methods: that on appropriate stimulation the blood has a higher concentration of the active substance in the vein draining the gland than in the artery supplying it. This technique is not usually practicable as the amounts of hormone released, even after stimulation, may be too small to be measured, either by biochemical or by bio-assay methods.

Bio-assay consists of testing the activity of the fluid which contains the substance to be measured by its specific action on animal tissues or living animals. The fluids commonly tested are blood and urine. As the concentration of the hormones is low in these fluids, it is sometimes advantageous to prepare concentrated extracts, but this introduces complications and difficulties. Even with the use of concentrated extracts of the fluid the test preparation may not be sufficiently sensitive to detect the hormone, either qualitatively or quantitatively. Biochemical estimations are likely to be more specific, but determinations of very small quantities are difficult. Great advances have been made in the estimation of adrenal cortical hormones by biochemical methods.

An indirect approach is to remove the tissue and show first that this loss results in a reproducible and predictable effect: that is, a specific function has been removed from the organism. Second, that administration of the active extract of the tissue to the animal deficient in this tissue restores it to normal. Third, that administration of the extract to the normal animal results in the opposite effects to the removal of the secreting tissue: this only applies to the main, or primary, action of the hormone. Commonly the tissue has the histological structure associated with secretory activity. These criteria must only be applied to normal tissue, as any cellular disorder could result in the release of active chemical substances into the blood stream. The sole observation that an extract of a tissue exerts a specific effect on administration is no evidence that this substance is normally released into the blood stream.

There is a group of organs which in the main do fulfil the described criteria, and have been accepted as being endocrine glands. These are the thyroid, parathyroids, the gonads, the islet tissue of the pancreas, the adrenals and the pituitary (or hypophysis). The adrenal and hypophysis each consist of two glands anatomically combined; the former is divided into the cortex and the medulla, and the latter into the adenohypophysis and the neurohypophysis. It must be accepted that the present classification is an arbitrary one and this is due to the manner in which the subject developed; this was based on clinical observations of the effects of disease of these organs. The roles of the pineal, spleen and thymus have yet to be settled and will only be briefly discussed, together with the placenta. When dealing with invertebrates it is not possible to apply the same criteria and this problem is con-considered in Chapter 15.

In the vertebrates, notably the mammals, there is a complex series of hormones released in the upper part of the alimentary canal. The function of these hormones is to stimulate the digestive glands of the stomach and pancreas, or to cause contraction of the gall bladder, or to inhibit both the motility and secretions of the stomach. Briefly, these hormones are released in the presence of partly digested protein, or hydrochloric acid, or fat, but there is also a nervous regulation of these secretions and movements of the digestive system. Hence a complete failure of the humoral mechanism will not result in any obvious change. Therefore it is not possible to apply the described criteria for establishing that the upper part of the alimentary canal is an endocrine gland. This has resulted in the paradox that, while it is accepted that a group of cells in the duodenum and stomach (their exact site is unknown) secrete hormones, these cells are not regarded as endocrine glands, despite the fact that secretin was the first hormone to be described. These alimentary hormones will only be considered briefly, as the main topic in the vertebrate section will be the hormones of the endocrine glands.

The majority of the ductless glands are present in all orders of vertebrates and a hormone administered from one class to another will usually exert its specific effect. The actions of the various endocrine glands are interrelated, so that they may be regarded as a functional system.

The effects of complete removal of the testes were described by Aristotle[11] in the fourth century B.C., and in the first century A.D. Dioscorides[26] recommended the testis of the white cock as a magical aid for the fathering of male children. Accurate studies of the endocrine glands did not, however, commence until the middle of the nineteenth century. The first significant experiment was made in 1849 by Berthold,[18] who removed and transplanted the gonads of birds and demonstrated that the testes had another function besides that of spermatogenesis. He suggested that the changes induced by castration were caused by the lack of some substance secreted by the testes and carried along by the blood stream.

The concept that certain organs such as the thyroid produced substances which enter the blood stream was first suggested by Ruysch (1690).[54] This important idea was overlooked and Bernard (1855)[16] received the credit for the somewhat revolutionary concept of chemical messengers circulating in the blood stream, as he introduced the term 'internal secretions'. However, Bernard was referring to the secretion of glucose by the liver and not to hormones.

A real stimulus to hormonal physiology came from astute clinicians, in particular the careful description by Addison (1868)[8] of the disease which now bears his name. He demonstrated that this disease followed destruction of the suprarenals. At that time it was believed that many of the diseases of man associated with changes in the tissues which are now called endocrine glands were due to errors in the natural processes of rendering toxins harmless.

That there are tissues which elaborate chemical messengers was apparently first clearly advanced by Brown-Séquard and d'Arsonval (1891).[19] Popular interest had been aroused in this subject by the claim of Brown-Séquard (1889)[19] that administration of testicular extracts had a rejuvenating effect on man. Subsequently it was shown that these preparations were inert and the remarkable effects observed must have been induced by suggestion.

The methods of control of the secretions of the hormones were not discovered until this century when Aschner (1912)[12] first showed that hypophysectomy (removal of the pituitary) caused atrophy of the genital organs of the dog. Evans and Long (1922)[27] found that rats treated with pituitary extracts had enlarged ovaries. Similarly it was demonstrated by other workers at about the same time that the control of the thyroid and adrenal cortex was by the pituitary. Of the other endocrine glands, the nervous control of the adrenal medulla was long known and a similar mechanism was shown to exist for the posterior pituitary.[28] The secretions of the islets of Langerhans and parathyroids are considered to be directly controlled by the blood level of glucose and calcium respectively. The factors influencing the secretion of the adenohypophysis were for a considerable time shrouded in mystery. It is now believed that nervous tissue in close proximity to the pituitary gland elaborates chemical substances which reach this gland by a local network of blood vessels, and control its secretory activity. Thus the central nervous system, either directly or indirectly, controls the majority of endocrine glands.

The identification of the structural formulae of those hormones, which are steroids, or modified amino acids, or simple polypeptides, is complete; the structure of the remaining hormones, which are more complex polypeptides, has still to be elucidated. Probably all hormones circulating in the blood are to a large extent bound to proteins, and there is a dynamic equilibrium between these two forms. It is likely that the tissues can only utilize the unbound form and when this occurs a proportion of the hormone is freed from the protein to restore the equilibrium. As far as is known, hormones do not initiate chemical processes, but regulate them. As a general rule, the endocrine glands secrete a basal quantity of the appropriate hormone to maintain the constancy of the internal environment of the organism.

2

The pituitary gland

THE anatomical position of the pituitary body is basically the same in all tetrapod vertebrates, an ovoid structure lying in the centre of the base of the skull, almost completely surrounded by bone. A short stalk connects the pituitary body to the under-surface of the brain. The body is subdivided into the adeno-hypophysial and the neurohypophysial components. The former consists of three parts: the pars distalis (which corresponds to the anterior pituitary of the old terminology), and behind this is the pars intermedia, while the pars tuberalis partially encircles the pituitary stalk. The neurohypophysis is a protrusion from the ventral wall of the hypothalamus. Into it there pass numerous nerve fibres, the majority of which appear to be derived from large nerve cells lying in the paired supraoptic and paraventricular nuclei. Most of these fibres end in the expanded distal portion of the neurohypophysis, the infundibular process (pars nervosa), which in most classes is in part ensheathed by the pars intermedia of the adenohypophysis. The two together comprise the posterior lobe of the pituitary gland. To innervate the infundibular process the nerve fibres traverse first the median eminence of the neuro-hypophysis, and then the infundibular stem, definitely innervat-ing blood vessels in the former, and possibly in the latter too. These two components of the neurohypophysis are also partly ensheathed in many classes by the pars tuberalis of the adenohypo-physis (Fig. 1). Interestingly enough, however, there are classes in which pars tuberalis or pars intermedia appear to be absent.

The adenohypophysis arises from an upgrowth from the primitive mouth while the stalk and pars nervosa are derived from a downgrowth from the brain. The pars intermedia is

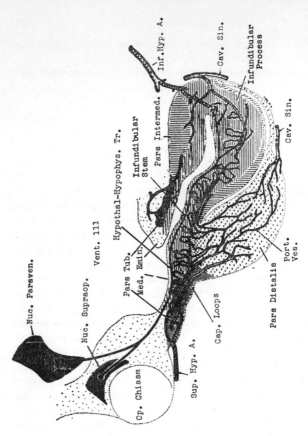

Op. Chiasm. = Optic Chiasma
Sup. Hyp. A. = Superior Hypo-
    physial Artery
Cap. Loops = Capillary Loops
Port. Ves. = Portal Vessel
Cav. Sin. = Cavernous Sinus
Inf. Hyp. A. = Inferior Hypophysial
    Artery
Pars Tub. = Pars Tuberalis
Med. Emin. = Median Eminence
Hypothal-Hypophys. Tr. = Hypo-
    thalamic-Hypophysial Tract
Vent. III = Ventricle III
Nuc. Supraop. = Supraoptic
    Nucleus
Nuc. Paraven. = Paraventricular
    Nucleus

(Reproduced from J. A. Russell in Ruch and Fulton's *A Textbook of Physiology* ed. 18. Philadelphia, W. B. Saunders Company, 1960; this diagram was drawn by Dr H. W. Ades)

Fig. 1 A schematic illustration of a mammalian pituitary body and part of the hypothalamic area

briefly mentioned in the section on mammals and the role of this gland on pigmentation in the poikilothermic vertebrates is given in Chapter 10. As the pars tuberalis has no known hormonal activity, only a passing reference is made to this structure.

1 Adenohypophysis

MAMMALS

The pars distalis of the adenohypophysis is believed to be responsible for the secretion of all the hormones derived from this structure. In most vertebrates three types of cell can be distinguished with the haemotoxylin and eosin staining technique, chromophobe (agranular), and chromophil (granular), the latter being eosinophilic or basophilic. It is possible to distinguish two types of eosinophil and basophil cells. In addition, chromophobes are subdivided into large and small.

The hormones secreted by the adenohypophysis may be divided into those which control the secretion of other endocrine glands and are named trophic (or tropic) hormones; the remainder act without the mediation of another endocrine gland. Trophic hormones not only control the formation and the release of the appropriate hormone from the respective endocrine gland, but are also responsible for the cellular activity and growth of that gland. There is evidence that the trophic hormones may induce changes directly in some non-endocrine tissues.

It is believed that the basophil cells secrete the trophic hormones controlling the gonads and the thyroid, and that the eosinophil cells secrete growth hormone and prolactin. The site of production of the trophic hormone controlling the adrenal cortex is still in doubt. It would appear that the small chromophobes are capable of secreting all the trophic hormones.

The gonadotrophic hormones are the follicle-stimulating hormone (FSH), which in the female is responsible for the maturation and development of the ovarian follicle, and the luteinizing hormone (LH) which controls the formation of the mammalian corpus luteum in the ovary. A third hormone luteotrophin (LTH) may be necessary to stimulate the corpus luteum to secrete its hormone.

In adult females of the higher primates the following cycle of events occurs. The adenohypophysis secretes FSH in increasing amounts and this hormone induces ripening of the ovarian follicle which in turn secretes oestradiol. Oestradiol acts on the adenohypophysis directly, or indirectly, to decrease the amount of FSH secreted. If the level of FSH falls it is suggested that the second gonadotrophic hormone LH will be secreted. At some critical blood concentration of these two trophic hormones rupture of the follicle is induced with release of the ovum. After ovulation blood levels of LH increase which induce the development of a corpus luteum, but it may be that this will only secrete progesterone if sufficient LTH reaches it. As the corpus luteum matures, increasing amounts of progesterone are produced which depress the output of LH and LTH. Now insufficient trophic hormones are secreted to maintain the corpus luteum, which then atrophies, and the main source of progesterone is removed. If the output of LH and LTH falls, the adenohypophysis will secrete FSH and another follicle is stimulated. While the negative feedback action of progesterone on LH is accepted, this may not apply to LTH in all classes of mammals; in the rat, progesterone may stimulate LTH secretion.

In man, both the follicle and the corpus luteum each ripen and degenerate in a period of two weeks. The whole cycle of events therefore lasts about one month and is repeated throughout the reproductive life of the female. It is only at puberty that the ovaries respond to gonadotrophins and it is suggested that the adenohypophysis is producing FSH, so the first cycle, when it commences, begins with a ripening follicle. Once started the cycles (menstrual cycles) will continue until either there are no more ova in the ovaries or until the latter no longer respond to gonadotrophins.

In the mammals below primates the mature female does not exhibit these menstrual changes, but at some period sufficient FSH is secreted to induce ripening of the ovarian follicle which in turn produces oestradiol: only at this period will the female accept the male. The duration and frequency of these periods of 'heat' vary in different mammals. Some have only one a year and others may have many.[29]

In the male, FSH is responsible for the maturation of the spermatozoa in the tubules of the testis, a trophic hormone acting on non-endocrine tissue. Interstitial cell stimulating hormone (ICSH) which is identical to LH controls the secretion of testosterone, a hormone secreted by specialized (interstitial) cells which are found between the tubules. In the male the adenohypophysis does not secrete FSH and LH alternately but simultaneously, as apparently the concentration of testosterone never reaches a level high enough to suppress the secretion of LH, and there is no hormone produced in response to FSH.

As removal of the pituitary gland leads not only to a deficiency of gonadal hormones but also of adrenal cortical and thyroid hormones with atrophy of these glands, it is evident that adrenocorticotrophic hormone (ACTH) and thyrotrophic hormone (or thyroid stimulating hormone, TSH) are also secreted by the adenohypophysis. Further, administration of either thyroid or adrenal cortical hormone leads to atrophy of the appropriate endocrine gland, indicating that the secretion of the trophic hormone is suppressed (Chapters 3, 4 and 5). Hence, to induce an excess of these hormones it is necessary to administer an amount greater than the normal basal secretion.

The adenohypophysis also secretes hormones which control growth and which induce milk secretion by the breast tissue under suitable conditions. The hormone controlling the latter was known as prolactin, but it now appears that this may be identical to LTH. Prolactin (LTH) induces the secretion of milk by the mammary glands provided these glands have been previously sensitized by adequate amounts of oestradiol and progesterone. In women, on rare occasions at parturition, the pituitary gland is destroyed by some disease process; in these circumstances the breasts fail to secrete milk. The growth hormone, also referred to as somatotrophin (STH), not only controls the rate of growth, but also the metabolism necessary for this growth.

Evidence that the pituitary gland controls growth is given by the following observations. Hypophysectomy prevents growth in the young animal and no combination of other hormones will then induce growth. Injection of adenohypophysial extracts restores the animal to normal, and if these extracts are given to the young normal animal excessive growth can be induced. In the child underactivity or overactivity of the adenohypophysis may occur, and dwarfism or gigantism respectively will be induced. Human dwarfs will only respond to growth hormones prepared from the pituitary glands of man or monkey; the hormone responsible for growth has been isolated.

Extracts of the adenohypophysis have been shown to promote gluconeogenesis (the conversion of proteins and fats to glucose, or a substance that can be metabolized in place of glucose; either mechanism results in a rise of the blood glucose level). Indeed, it seems that the adenohypophysis is necessary for the metabolism of all foodstuffs. In addition, it was found that repeated injections of a crude extract of the pituitary gland into dogs would induce permanent diabetes mellitus (Chapter 7) by destroying the islet tissue. Subsequently it was reported that this change would only occur in the fully grown animal and it is believed that the diabetogenic action is mainly due to the growth hormone. Not all mammals respond in the same manner: rats are relatively resistant, possibly because growth is continuous throughout life. A possible mechanism by which STH exerts its diabetogenic action is that insulin is needed to control growth, and excessive amounts of STH overstimulate the β cells of the islets of Langerhans leading to their eventual destruction. Further, adenohypophysial extracts will stimulate gluconeogenesis directly, and indirectly by virtue of the ACTH present which will increase the output of adrenal cortical hormones. In crude extracts the so-called diabetogenic factor probably consists of a mixture of STH and ACTH. Finally it has been claimed that a factor (possibly STH) from the adenohypophysis will inhibit glucose uptake by the tissues.

Adenohypophysial hormones are polypeptides (groups of amino acids) which are bound to proteins, and only recently has it been possible to separate them from the protein part. The molecular weight of the adenohypophysial hormones varies between 25,000 and 100,000. Whether the hormones are normally secreted by the gland in a protein bound form is unknown, but it is likely that this is the manner in which they circulate in the blood stream.

A hormone secreted by the pars intermedia is known as melanocyte stimulating hormone (MSH), or sometimes referred to as intermedin. Reference is made to β MSH in mammals, as in the pig an additional hormone has been isolated and is referred to as α MSH: β MSH is a complex polypeptide which in man consists of twenty-two amino acids. All classes of vertebrates appear to possess this hormone, but it is likely that it is only of functional importance in the poikilothermic vertebrates (Chapter 10). In man this hormone increases melanin synthesis in the melanophore cells and thus the skin darkens. While it is possible to extract this substance from the pituitary glands of mammals, its function is still uncertain. Some mammals, namely the Indian elephant and the whale, do not possess a discrete pars intermedia. The molecular structures of MSH and ACTH are closely related, and therefore it is not surprising that on administration even highly purified preparations of ACTH lead to darkening of the skin.

There is good evidence that the hypothalamus, an area of the brain immediately above the pituitary gland, controls the secretion of gonadotrophins by the adenohypophysis in all classes above fish; it is likely that ACTH and TSH are similarly controlled. Evidence in favour of this is that electrical stimulation of the appropriate area of the hypothalamus leads to an increased output of gonadotrophic hormones, whereas direct stimulation of the adenohypophysis is ineffective. Destruction of particular sites in this region of the brain results in a diminished output of the trophic hormones.

In the vertebrates above the fish a specialized area of the hypothalamus, known as the median eminence, develops; capillaries from this area of the brain supply the pars distalis. The current belief is that the hypothalamic control of the adenohypophysis is not achieved by a neural mechanism, but by chemical messengers which are carried to it by these special blood vessels. Thus the median eminence plays an essential role in connecting the central nervous system with the pars distalis, and the importance of this structure in the evolution of vertebrates has been well summarized.[1] Evidence in favour of chemical transmission is the observation that cutting the pituitary stalk only induces a temporary loss of secretory activity by the adenohypophysis, whereas if the blood vessels in the stalk are prevented from joining up, the loss is permanent. Further, if the pituitary gland is removed and transplanted elsewhere, the normal cyclical changes of the female no longer occur. There is still doubt as to whether the latter procedure leads to any marked impairment of function of the adrenal cortex or thyroid. If the pituitary gland is transplanted back to its original site gonadal function is restored. An interesting experiment which illustrates that the hypothalamus controls the sexual cycles of lower mammals is as follows. The pituitary gland of the female can be successfully replaced by one from the male of the same species, whereas a castrate male, with the pituitary gland intact, does not show cyclical sex changes if ovaries are implanted. It was suggested that the hormones of the pars nervosa may be the chemical messengers, as these hormones are released in the median eminence and they do cause stimulation of the adenohypophysis, but only in very large doses. It is now believed that whatever the nature of the chemical messenger, its formula is likely to be similar to that of the neurohypophysial hormones. A chemical substance—a polypeptide—has been isolated from the hypothalamus which causes the release of ACTH.

The cyclical alterations of sexual activity observed in mammals below primates, and those to be described for other vertebrates, are apparently determined by changes in output of gonadotrophic hormones. While it is possible that there is some internal rhythm regulating these changes, it seems likely that alterations of the external environment influence the activity of the hypothalamus which controls the rate of secretion of gonadotrophins by the adenohypophysis. It would thus appear that an inherent rhythm is monitored by the external environment and this would explain why the breeding seasons occur at particular times of the year. Important external factors are the intensity and duration of the light reaching the animal. In the ferret it would appear that light stimuli are relayed to the hypothalamus by the optic nerves, but in birds it seems that the light may be conducted through the eyes and the skull bones to act directly on the hypothalamus. Other external factors of some importance are temperature changes, rainfall, or alterations of odour due to different types of vegetation.

The higher primates which can breed at any time are apparently free of external environmental control and the menstrual cycle is determined by the inherent regular changes of secretion of FSH and LH. Evolution has therefore produced a class which is independent of the vagaries of the external environment—a valuable advance, although man has not yet completely broken away from the shackles of outside controls. Emotional upsets and changes of habit may alter the menstrual cycle, and the libido of man is often greatly influenced by environmental factors.

BIRDS

The adenohypophysis consists of a pars distalis (which can be further subdivided into a cephalic and a caudal portion in which there are eosinophilic and basophilic cells) and a pars tuberalis, but there is no discrete pars intermedia.

Probably the pituitary glands of birds, like those of mammals, possess ACTH, TSH and gonadotrophins, the basophil cells being responsible for the secretion of the latter. The existence of the growth hormone has yet to be established in this class of vertebrates. It is true that hypophysectomy retards the growth of the young, but normal growth is restored by the administration of LTH. To the clinician an observation which is of interest is that administration of TSH to ducklings is found to induce protrusion of the eyes.

In pigeons administration of LTH stimulates the crop sac and, by desquamation of degenerate cells, crop milk is formed: this hormone also has an insulin-antagonizing action. The gonads of both sexes in fowls and pigeons are inhibited by LTH which probably acts by suppressing the secretion of gonadotrophins. It is likely that the post-breeding gonadal regression is due to this hormone. While LTH is responsible for broodiness in hens and pigeons, the maternal behaviour and regurgitation feeding habits are, in part, genetically determined. In the perching birds the formation of the incubation patch is to some degree controlled by the blood level of LTH. Hence, there are many examples of LTH (a trophic hormone) acting directly on non-endocrine tissue. It has been suggested that the redhead duck (*Aythya americana*) which lays its eggs in other birds' nests may lack this hormone.

The effects of hypophysectomy are more serious than in mammals, and death occurs unless the fall of blood glucose after the operation is prevented. This procedure as with other vertebrates results in atrophy of the thyroid, adrenal cortex and gonads, and, because of the changes in the latter organ, the accessory sex organs degenerate. In addition, there is atrophy of the small intestine, liver and pancreas, and in pigeons the crop sac also shrinks. The general activity of the birds is reduced and the food and water consumptions decrease, associated with a fall of body temperature and metabolic rate; there is precipitation of a moult.

As in the mammal, the hypothalamus probably controls the secretion of adenohypophysial gonadotrophins by chemical transmitters, but whether this applies to the other adenohypophysial hormones is doubtful.

REPTILES

There is a great variation in the anatomy of the pituitary gland in reptiles and it is asymmetrical in lizards (*Xantusia*), the pars nervosa and intermedia being displaced to the right of the centre. The pars intermedia is larger than in any other class and the pars tuberalis may be absent. In general this gland is very similar to that of the amphibians.

Hypophysectomy is relatively easy to perform in snakes, but extremely difficult in lizards. The results of this procedure in snakes reveal that the pituitary gland is responsible for maturation of the spermatozoa and the general function of the testes and in the female for the maturation of the ovarian follicles and maintenance of the stroma. In those classes where viviparity (the birth of freely mobile young) occurs, it is still uncertain whether hypophysectomy results in resorption of the embryos. This procedure certainly prevents ovulation.

It appears that the gonads of reptiles will respond to mammalian preparations of gonadotrophins FSH, LH and LTH. It is likely that the adenohypophysis not only secretes gonadotrophins but in addition ACTH and TSH.

AMPHIBIANS

The pars distalis is well developed and the pars intermedia is on its antero-dorsal margin. The amphibians are apparently the earliest vertebrate class which possess a pars tuberalis and it may be separate from the pars distalis. The pars nervosa shows considerable variation in the different classes of the amphibians and may only consist of a plate of cells.

In the pars distalis two types of eosinphils and two types of basophils are recognized. It is generally agreed that the basophils are the source of gonadotrophins. Hypophysectomy leads to degeneration of the gonads and these will regenerate if the pituitary gland is re-implanted, but apparently somatic growth is unaffected by the procedure. In the male the gonadotrophic hormones are not only responsible for the normal development of spermatozoa and for the maintenance of the interstitial cells of the testes but also for the expulsion of the spermatozoa to the exterior. In the female gonadotrophins are responsible for ovulation and for the maintenance of ovarian function, but there is a seasonal variation in the sensitivity of the ovarian tissue to the trophic hormones. It is accepted that the pars distalis contains both TSH and ACTH. It has been claimed that in the salamander LTH increases the water drive, and a return to water is essential for successful procreation. This unusual action of LTH allows interesting speculations to be made on the evolutionary functions of hormones.

Mammalian sources of gonadotrophins are effective in inducing spermiation and ovulation. This forms the basis of the amphibian test for pregnancy in women.

FISHES

In fishes the pituitary gland is conveniently divided into three portions: the anterior, which is possibly comparable to the pars tuberalis of higher vertebrates, the middle and posterior lobes corresponding to the pars distalis and pars intermedia respectively. Closely associated with the posterior portion of the adenohypophysis (pars intermedia), and extending into it, is the pars nervosa; the term neuro-intermediate lobe is often applied to this region. In the teleosts strands of the pars nervosa may come into intimate contact with all parts of the adenohypophysis. Unlike the other classes, the blood supply to the parsmervosa is not separate from the adenohypophysis and there is no portal supply from the hypothalamus to the pars distalis. It has been suggested that the neurohypophysial hormones may act as regulators of adenohypophysial secretion.

As in mammals, the cells of the middle lobe can be divided into two types, eosinophils and basophils, as revealed by the haemotoxylin and eosin stains.

Observations made on normal and on hypophysectomized animals, with or without injections of adenohypophysial hormones, have indicated that the pituitary gland contains growth hormone, LTH, FSH, ACTH and TSH. These vertebrates respond to mammalian growth hormone, ACTH and TSH, but are relatively unresponsive to mammalian gonadotrophic hormones. However, the reverse does not always apply, in that mammals do not usually respond to adenohypophysial extracts of fish, possibly because the extracts are in a crude form. It may be that biochemical differences exist between fish and mammalian adenohypophysial hormones, or the active molecular groups are the same but the protein to which they are bound is different.

There is some relationship between ACTH secretion and the growth of fishes, as under conditions of stress, when ACTH secretion is increased, there is impaired growth. It has been suggested that an excess of ACTH inhibits the secretion of growth hormone. There is evidence that LTH is important for oviposition in some of the fishes.

It appears likely that the pituitary gland of fishes secretes a hormone, or hormones, which promote gluconeogenesis, as removal of the gland results in a fall of the blood glucose level and of the glycogen stores. The pituitary glands of some classes of fish control the level of blood electrolytes. In killifish (*Fundulus*) hypophysectomy results in a fall in the level of the plasma chlorides and injections of all known adenohypophysial hormones are ineffective, but administration of an extract of the pituitary gland of the killifish prolongs the survival time. Hypophysectomy in the eel leads to a fall of the blood calcium level, but the chloride concentration is unaffected.

It would appear that the activity of the pituitary gland is necessary for the migration of eels. Lastly, it should be emphasized that the effects of hypophysectomy in fishes are of gradual onset, when compared with mammals.

The pituitary gland possesses a melanophore-concentrating factor possibly derived from the anterior glandular portion which induces pallor of the skin, and this factor may be a hormone; while in the posterior lobe (pars intermedia) there is MSH (Chapter 10). It seems that LTH is essential for melanin synthesis in *Fundulus*.

It is accepted that the pituitary gland controls the hormones secreted by the ovaries, and that in turn the ovarian hormones control the secretion of gonadotrophins: ovulation is determined by the level of LH in the blood. As it is unlikely that progesterone is secreted by the ovaries of fish, it would seem that the function of LH in inducing ovulation is phylogenetically much older than its probable additional role in mammals of developing and maintaining a corpus luteum.

2 Neurohypophysis

The gland can be conveniently considered under one heading and not as elsewhere under the different vertebrate classes. The basic action of one of the two hormones, vasopressin or an analogous substance, is apparently the same in all terrestrial vertebrates, namely the maintenance of the osmotic tension of the extracellular fluid, and indirectly that of the intracellular fluid. The second hormone, oxytocin, appears to exert its action only in mammals, but it may play some part in oviposition in the other vertebrates.

At the end of the nineteenth century it was found that in

mammals an extract of the pars nervosa (or posterior lobe as it was then called) raised the blood pressure.[52] Subsequently it was found that these extracts also induced contractions of the uterus and it was suggested that this substance might be an important stimulus to the uterus at birth and hence it was named oxytocin (derived from oxytocic, meaning quick labour).[24] Thus there were two principles in the pars nervosa, vasopressor (an elevator of blood pressure) and oxytocic. Experiments at the beginning of the twentieth century suggested that there was a third principle which resulted in an increase of urine volume and was referred to as a diuretic factor (diuresis means to increase urine flow). Later it was realized that this observation was due to poor control of the experimental procedures, and under satisfactory conditions an antidiuretic factor (antidiuresis is a fall in urine flow) was present.[62] It is now apparent that the antidiuretic factor and the blood pressure raising factor are one substance. It is unlikely that the vasopressor action plays any part in the control of the blood pressure, but the antidiuretic effect is of great functional importance in the maintenance of water balance. Thus reference is sometimes made to antidiuretic hormone (ADH), but it is preferable to refer to this hormone as vasopressin. It would appear that haemorrhage does result in the release of extra amounts of vasopressin, but not in sufficient quantities to elevate the blood pressure; the hormonal action is to conserve water.

It is agreed that the hormones oxytocin and vasopressin which are found in the pars nervosa are probably elaborated in nerve cells of the paraventricular and supraoptic nuclei of the hypothalamus and in the nerve fibres. These fibres end mainly in the pars nervosa in close proximity to capillaries, and some terminate in the median eminence and infundibulum; the hormones are released from these nerve endings. In view of this, vasopressin and oxytocin are referred to as neurohypophysial hormones.

The kidney is made up of nephrons. Each nephron consists of a glomerulus where the plasma is filtered and a tubule which selectively re-absorbs substances, so that the final product is urine. In mammals vasopressin acts on the distal part of the kidney tubules and promotes the re-absorption of water. If an excess of this hormone is present, the urine volume falls and the specific gravity rises. Verney (1947),[63] in a series of elegant experiments, showed that the factor controlling the secretion of vasopressin was the sodium chloride concentration of the blood which is usually increased when there is a deficiency of water. If this concentration rises above normal, the rate of secretion of vasopressin increases and more water is retained by the kidney. Sufficient water is retained to restore the sodium chloride concentration; the stimulus to the gland is removed, and the urine flow returns to normal. A fall of sodium chloride concentration, as occurs when there is an excess of water, inhibits the secretion of vasopressin and the urine flow increases above normal; sufficient water is lost to restore once more the sodium choloride level. Hence even under resting conditions some vasopressin is secreted. This mechanism which responds to changes of sodium chloride level is able to maintain the fluid balance of the organism within narrow limits.

Absence of, or damage to, the pars nervosa leads to a profuse diuresis and this disorder of man is called diabetes insipidus; in this condition the urine volume may be as high as fifteen pints a day. A similar state can be induced experimentally in mammals by removing the pars nervosa, or by cutting the nerve fibres connecting it to the hypothalamus. If the adenohypophysis is removed with the pars nervosa, diabetes insipidus is not induced. It was suggested that the adenohypophysis secreted a diuretic hormone which opposed the antidiuretic action of vasopressin. It is likely, however, that the effect of hypophysectomy is indirect, in that following the removal of this gland the adrenal cortex atrophies; a deficiency of adrenal cortical hormones always induces a fall of urine volume which will not increase even if the water intake is increased. Therefore, in the presence of a deficiency of both vasopressin and adrenal cortical hormones, the changes in urine volume are small.

Until recently it was believed that oxytocin played no real part at parturition (birth of the young) because it had been shown that in mammals, if the pars nervosa was absent, there was no apparent difficulty in the birth of the young.[32] It was suggested that after removal or destruction of the pars nervosa, although diabetes insipidus results, sufficient oxytocin secreting cells remain to allow parturition to proceed normally. Indirect observation and bio-assay of oxytocin in the blood have shown that the concentration of the hormone rises at labour. The concept has been advanced that this hormone is necessary for parturition,[20] but it is more likely that its role is only a minor one.

An important function of oxytocin is to expel the milk from the lactating mammary glands. It has been demonstrated that the young do not suck the milk when suckling, but that it is expelled into their mouths. As the result of stimulation of the nipple area by the infant's lips, nervous impulses are relayed into the spinal cord and thence to the hypothalamus. Oxytocin is secreted in response to this nervous stimulation and reaches the breast by the blood stream. This hormone not only causes contraction of the smooth muscle of the ducts but also the specialized cells which surround the secreting cells of the gland. Thus the ejection of milk at suckling, or the 'let-down' of milk as it is referred to by agricultural workers, is a neurohormonal reflex.[23] Adrenaline, a hormone of the adrenal medulla, secreted under conditions of fear and stress, inhibits this reflex. It is now readily apparent why the infant of the frightened mother is unable to obtain milk and the inexperienced worker may find milking a cow difficult.[23]

The role of oxytocin in the non-pregnant female and in the male has yet to be elucidated. Another problem is whether the neurohypophysial hormones can be secreted separately: for example, does the female have an antidiuresis at parturition or whenever the young suckle? Similarly, if the sodium chloride concentration of the blood is elevated, is oxytocin secreted in addition to vasopressin, and would this therefore induce uterine contraction in the pregnant animal, or milk ejection in the lactating female? There is some evidence that there may be independent release of these hormones in man.

The structural formulae of vasopressin and oxytocin have been established and the hormones synthesized. They are octapeptide amides. Vasopressin differs from oxytocin only in two of its amino acids. If phenylalanine and arginine replace isoleucine and leucine respectively, oxytocin is converted to vasopressin (Fig. 2). As is to be expected from the similarity of the formulae,

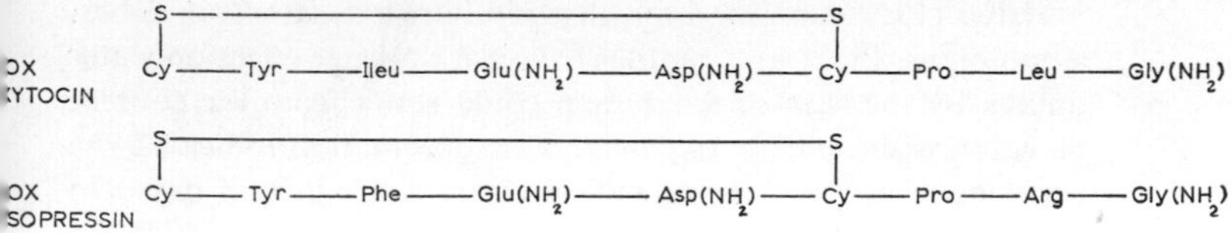

S — S
Cy.......Cy = Cystine   Tyr = Tyrosine   Ileu = Isoleucine
$Glu(NH_2)$ = Glutamine $Asp(NH_2)$ = Asparagine   Pro = Proline
Leu = Leucine $Gly(NH_2)$ = Glycinamide   Phe = Phenylalanine
Arg = Arginine

Fig. 2 The amino acid sequence of the neurohypophysial hormones. The close relationship of the two hormones is apparent

vasopressin exerts some oxytocic effect, and oxytocin possesses slight antidiuretic activity. The structural formula of vasopressin is the same in all mammals except in the pig and the hippopotamus, where the amino acid arginine is replaced by lysine.

Only in mammals and possibly in birds may the urine be hypertonic to plasma, thus providing an important mechanism in the conservation of water. In the other vertebrates the maximum concentration of the urine that can be achieved is isotonic with plasma, and other mechanisms may play a part in fluid balance. One such mechanism which occurs in amphibians is the water uptake by the skin. It has been shown that neurohypophysial hormones increase the uptake of water in the frog, but the action is mainly due to oxytocin. This movement of water through the skin will only occur if the body fluids are hypertonic to the external environment. Further, oxytocin, by reducing the rate of glomerular filtration by the kidney, does reduce the urine volume. Another mechanism is the re-absorption of water by the bladder, and this process is significantly affected by neurohypophysial hormones. Recently it has been shown that in frogs vasopressin acts on the kidney tubules, increasing the uptake of water.

Heller (1950)[33] pointed out that pituitary extracts from fishes, amphibians, birds and reptiles have a far greater effect on water uptake by the skin of frogs than could result from the content of vasopressin and/or oxytocin. This observation indicated the presence of another unknown hormone. Analogues of oxytocin have been prepared synthetically and one, vasotocin, in which the leucine of oxytocin is replaced by arginine, has far greater activity in increasing the water uptake by frogs than either of the neuro-hypophysial hormones of mammals. It now appears likely that the neurohypophysial hormones of amphibians, reptiles, birds and some teleost fish are vasotocin (in place of vasopressin) and oxytocin.[49] As vasopressin is present in the pituitary body of marsupials,[56] it would appear that this hormone made its appearance very early in mammalian evolution, or was present in the now non-existent reptilian stock from which mammals are descended.

In birds it seems likely that vasotocin functions in exactly the same fashion as vasopressin in mammals in the conservation of water. Lesions of the hypothalamus in the hen lead to excessive drinking of water and a diuresis. Isotocin, a quite distinct octa-peptide, has been found in the pituitary gland of some teleost fish, but, in the elasmobranch, hormones different from any known neurohypophysial hormones, or their analogues, appear to be present. The role of neurohypophysial hormones in fish has yet to be clarified, but they may be responsible for initiating spawning in some of the teleosts; in amphibians they are probably important in maintaining the water balance through the skin.

In the evolution of the neurohypophysial hormones it would not be unreasonable to conjecture that an octapeptide was the original hormone. The structure of this hormone was altered to isotocin early in the development of the vertebrates, probably in the teleost, and subsequently it was amended to vasotocin and oxytocin. These remained the neurohypophysial hormones until the mammalian class was reached, when vasopressin replaced vasotocin and the complex difficulties involved in the birth and nu-trition of the newborn resulted in oxytocin taking over the spec-ialized function of aiding these processes. In birds and reptiles it is suggested that oxytocin may be responsible for oviposition

Summary

The mammalian adenohypophysis was the first to be studied, and subsequent work on the other vertebrates has been a little clouded, because automatically attempts were made to compare these classes with the mammals. In all classes of vertebrates, extracts of the adenohypophysis possess many similar hormones, but this finding does not imply that they have the same action in all the classes. An excellent example of a hormone having an entirely different action in one class compared to the others is given by LTH, which in salamanders increases the water drive essential for successful procreation. In the submammalian classes only the adenohypophysis of the amphibians has essentially the same function as that of the mammal; this could be true of the other vertebrates, but lack of information prevents an adequate comparison. A common feature throughout all vertebrate classes is that the adenohypophysis controls the gonads, but whether the gonadotrophic hormones are the same in each class of vertebrates has not yet been clarified; it is true that mammalian gonadotrophic hormones are more or less effective in all the vertebrates. Interesting differences occur in the birds, for only in this class is the gland essential for life, but it is not necessary for normal growth.

In this chapter it has been assumed that LTH and prolactin are identical, and that LTH in mammals may be responsible for the complete maturation of the corpus luteum and for its endocrine secretion; LH being mainly concerned with inducing ovulation. However, LH may have identical functions to LTH with respect to the ovaries.

Throughout the vertebrate series the development of the adenohypophysis is the same, namely by an upgrowth of cells from the primitive mouth of the embryo. The lamprey is no exception, as the structure which gives rise to this gland is a homologue of the upgrowth.

One of the most fascinating aspects of the adenohypophysis is the control of its secretion by the central nervous system. A current concept in the tetrapods is that chemical messengers are secreted in the region of the median eminence, entering small blood vessels there; these vessels re-form and continue onwards to supply the adenohypophysis. It is claimed that the median eminence is only found in this class and it has been defined as the area in which blood vessels re-form to supply the adenohypophysis.[1] The whole emphasis at present is focussed on the supreme importance of the median eminence in the control of adenohypophysial secretion. It is believed that this view may have to be modified, as blood flows to this gland from other areas, namely the pars nervosa. In fish the blood supply is derived almost entirely from the pars nervosa, and this structure comes into direct relationship with the adenohypophysis. This anatomical arrangement has led to the suggestion that the hormones of the pars nervosa function by controlling the adenohypophysis, particularly as no other definite action can be ascribed to them in this class. In the evolution of the vertebrates the suggested concept is that the median eminence of the tetrapods has taken over this function, while the pars nervosa secretes hormones which have a peripheral action. It must be recalled that the elasmobranch and teleost fishes, which have been extensively studied, are not in the direct line in the development of the tetrapods. However, the lungfish (*Dipnoi*), which are nearer to the main line of evolution of these, do apparently possess a median eminence. There is evidence that in the tetrapods the hormones of the pars nervosa can induce the adenohypophysis to secrete, but more likely the chemical messengers are closely related compounds secreted in and around the median eminence. The problem is that one must postulate a specific chemical messenger for each hormone secreted by the adenohypophysis, otherwise all the hormones would be secreted simultaneously. In short, it is widely accepted that the central nervous system controls the adenohypophysis, but the details by which this is achieved have yet to be fully elucidated.

Little information has been given about the chemical structure of the adenohypophysial hormones, but it should be pointed out that FSH, LH and TSH may be referred to as glycoproteins, as they contain carbohydrate. Details of their structure have been adequately given elsewhere.[3]

Classification of the various types of cells of the adenohypophysis have become complex, as attempts have been made to reclassify these cells in order to identify the particular hormones they secrete. This has been considered by Barrington.[1]

In mammals it is accepted that vasopressin is an important agent in the conservation of water, and the same is true in birds, but here the hormone is arginine vasotocin. These hormones, the rate of secretion of which is determined by the osmolarity of the extra-cellular fluid, promote the re-absorption of water by the kidneys. Only in the homoiothermic vertebrates is it possible for for the urine to be hypertonic to plasma: in the other vertebrates the maximum concentration that can be achieved is isotonicity. In the poikilothermic tetrapods, the neurohypophysis also controls water balance, but this is achieved by the altered uptake of water by several tissues, the skin, urinary bladder and the kidney. The action of these hormones in the fish is uncertain.

The most important action of oxytocin in the mammals is to induce the expulsion of milk from the lactating breast. The hormone may also aid the delivery of the foetus and placenta at parturition. In the other vertebrates it may play a part in oviposition. The role of oxytocin in the male in all classes is unknown. It seems likely in mammals that oxytocin and vasopressin can be secreted independently. The neurohypophysis is unique in vertebrate endocrinology in that the hormones are elaborated in the nerve cells and/or their processes. This implies that nerve fibres are capable of both conducting and secreting chemical substances, or as it is now called, neurosecretion. The neurohypophysial hormones are released in close proximity to small blood vessels which allow both easy and rapid access to the blood stream. Thus, this gland is comparable to the neurohaemal organs of the invertebrates.

3

The gonads

SUBSTANCES that are responsible for male development and maintenance are referred to as androgens and in the majority of classes the naturally occurring hormone is testosterone. Similarly, feminizing hormones are referred to as oestrogens and in most classes the naturally occurring one is oestradiol.

The primary difference between the two sexes is determined by the gonads which are either ovaries or testes. In the embryo the sex chromosomes determine the development of the undifferentiated gonads, each of which consists of a medulla and a cortex, the medulla giving rise to the testis and the cortex to the ovary. The differentiated gonads secrete specific hormones which may be identical to those produced in adult life. If the testes develop, then the male hormone secreted is responsible for the further development of the Wolffian ducts into the epididymides and the vasa deferentia which open to the exterior directly, or indirectly by means of the urethra. The genital tubercle in male mammals develops into a penis and in a high proportion a superficial bag, or scrotum, forms, into which the testes eventually descend. If the foetal gonads are ovaries the hormones of this tissue are responsible for the development of the Müllerian ducts into the fallopian tubes, uterus (or uteri) and upper part of the vagina, while the genital tubercle in mammals forms the lower part of the vagina, the clitoris and the external genitalia (Fig. 3). In the monotremata and all classes below, both the male and female have a cloaca into which opens the rectum, urethra and genital ducts. In mammals once the foetal hormones have initiated the growth of the appropriate accessory sex organs, their further development may be independent of hormones.

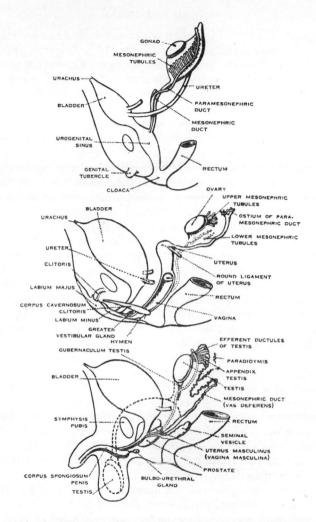

Fig. 3   The development of the genital tracts in mammals: undifferentiated stage (upper figure); adult female (middle); adult male (lower). The synonyms of the mesonephric and para-mesonephric ducts are the Wolffian and Müllerian ducts respectively

(Reproduced from *Textbook of Human Anatomy* (ed. W. J Hamilton) by the courtesy of Messrs Macmillan)

If the male mammalian embryo is castrated, then the development is that of a partial female; that is, the Müllerian instead of the Wolffian duct system develops, but in birds a different situation prevails in that the neuter condition is the male. Whether this is related to the fact that in birds, unlike mammals, the female is the digametic sex, is uncertain. If testosterone is given to the female embryo the growth of the Wolffian duct system is stimulated, leading to masculinization: similarly, oestrogen will stimulate the Müllerian duct system, feminizing the male embryo. At a certain stage of development it is possible, with the appropriate sex hormones, to reverse the sex in the tadpole, the chick, the opossum and possibly other mammals. Disorders of gonadal development will lead to abnormal development of either Wolffian or Müllerian ducts, and at birth the genital region may show any degree of variation from female to male and it may be difficult to determine the sex. Pseudohermaphroditism is a term used when the genital development is that of one sex and the gonads are of another; a true hermaphrodite has both ovaries and testes. Certain male teleosts may undergo sex change, revealing the bisexuality of the gonad.

An interesting sex alteration occurs in cattle. In some twinned foetuses the male member causes masculinization of the female and the latter is known as a freemartin. The freemartin, which is sterile, possesses testes and the genital ducts of a male, but the external genitals are female and in addition there are mammae: a similar condition may be found in pigs. It was suggested that this occurred because of the union of the foetal membranes and placenta which allowed the male hormones to enter the female foetus. This cannot be the complete answer; embryo male and female marmosets have a common placenta and yet there is no masculinization of the female.

In many vertebrates there is increased general activity at the time of the seasonal stimulation of the gonads. This may range from what appears to be random movements to highly organized migrations to the breeding grounds. Internal fertilization is universal in the amniotes, but external fertilization occurs in the majority of anamniotes. Viviparity is a characteristic of the placental and marsupial mammals, but some fishes, some reptiles and a few amphibians are viviparous, in which case the embryos are nurtured in the oviducts or ovaries. Pregnancy, or gestation, is the term used if the embryos are retained and develop inside the female. If some special structure forms, which allows nutrient material from the mother to pass to the embryo, it is called a placenta.

The gonads are the source of the gametes and secrete hormones which are responsible for the post-natal development of ducts that convey these gametes, and in addition for those characters which attract the opposite sex of its own class. In general the female is only a seasonal breeder, while the male in many classes of domesticated mammals may be sexually active at any time. Only a few examples of each class of vertebrates have been studied, and, perhaps wrongly, it has been assumed that they are truly representative of their class.

In the growth of the animal there is an interval before the accessory sex organs increase in size and the secondary sex characters appear; these are characteristic for each class. The accessory sex organs (Fig. 4) are the structures that aid in the transport of spermatozoa or ova, and are necessary for successful coitus; included with the accessory sex organs are those specialized glands whose secretions are essential for the survival of the gametes. The secondary sex characters are the body features which enable a distinction to be made between the sexes; some of these characters are developed to attract the opposite sex, and may aid in bringing the two bodies in close proximity during coitus. The distinction between accessory sex organs and secondary sex characters is somewhat artificial. The accessory sex organs are determined mainly by foetal gonadal hormones and in part by genetic constitution. The majority of secondary sex characters are under the control of adult gonadal hormones, with inborn factors regulating their sensitivity to these hormones.

There is little doubt that the mammalian ovary is capable of secreting androgens, but this androgen is different from testosterone. Whether this hormone is secreted normally, or only under special conditions, is not known. The testes secrete oestrogens, but their role in the physiological balance of the animal is not clear: it is of interest that the testes of the stallion are the

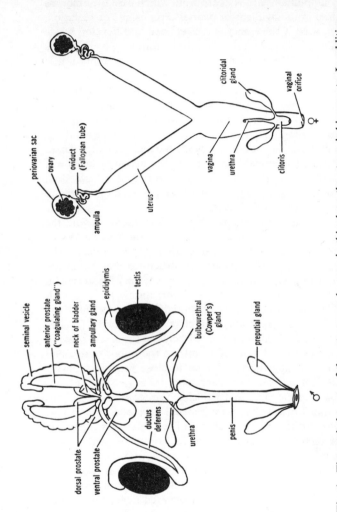

Fig. 4   The genital tracts of the rat; as can be seen in this class, the uterus is bicornuate. In addition to the accessory sex organs the gonads are shown, and in the female the position of the terminal part of the urethra

Reproduced from *A Textbook of Comparative Endocrinology* by Gorbman and Bern, by the courtesy of Messrs Wiley; this diagram is based on C. D. Turner, 1960)

richest source of oestrogens. Androgens and oestrogens are also secreted by the adrenal cortex.

1 The testes

Testis in Latin means a witness, and Roman law required this organ to be present before a man could give evidence as a witness; the word testimonial (the certificate of character) is derived from testis. The testes (or testicles) not only produce the spermatozoa but also secrete the hormone testosterone (Fig. 7). In man this hormone is secreted by well-differentiated cells (interstitial cells of Leydig), which are situated between the sperm-producing tubules. In the male, while the levels of LH and testosterone are inversely related, there is no corresponding hormonal control of FSH secretion, as this hormone only influences spermatogenesis. However, moderate quantities

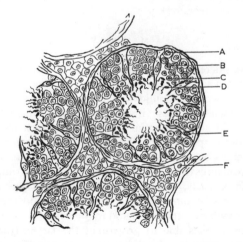

Fig. 5   Diagrammatic cross-section of mammalian testis

A = spermatogonia   B = primary spermatocytes
C = spermatids   D = spermatozoa   E = cells of Sertoli
F = interstitial cells of Leydig

of androgens will inhibit FSH secretion, and so depress spermato-genesis, but large doses have a direct stimulating action on the latter. In many classes of male vertebrates the testes also secrete some oestradiol (Fig. 7), or a similar substance, and one source of this is believed to be the supporting cells inside the tubules (Sertoli cells). Throughout the vertebrate classes the basic struc-ture of the testis is essentially similar (Fig. 5).

Miscellaneous information on androgens

Testosterone has, besides its masculinizing effect, an important action as a protein anabolizer (building up of amino acids to proteins), and absence of this hormone will result in excess pro-tein catabolism (breakdown of proteins to amino acids). Andro-genic activity can be estimated simply by measuring the 17-keto-steroids (androgens are excreted as 17-ketosteroids) in the urine, as these substances give a purple colour with an alcoholic solution of metadinitrobenzene and alcoholic potassium hydroxide (Zimmermann reaction).

MAMMALS

Man is considered as an example of the primate class. Between the ages of ten and eighteen years the accessory sex organs, name-ly the penis, scrotum, epididymis, prostate, seminal vesicles and Cowper's gland, increase in size. The latter three structures probably add some essential constituents which increase the viability of the spermatozoa. The seminal fluid (semen) refers to the fluid emission on orgasm, and consists of the fluid secretions of these structures (mainly from the seminal vesicles) and usually, but not necessarily, contain spermatozoa. Also the secondary sex characters become obvious, hair appears on the body (a profuse growth over the pubis and in the axilla) and on the faces The voice deepens due to growth of the larynx (the Adam'. apple) and muscular development increases. These changes are brought about by an increase in the rate of secretion of testosterone induced by a larger output of LH, and possibly due to the increased sensitivity of the interstitial cells of Leydig to this hormone. In addition, the testes themselves increase in size. The acquisition of the secondary sex characters and the growth of the accessory sex organs are referred to as puberty. At this time there are marked mental changes and the sex drive becomes obvious; whereas previously the male preferred male company, he now becomes interested in the female. The change in the mental approach, together with what is referred to as the typical aggressiveness of the male, is, in part, due to testosterone, but social custom may be an important factor. In some communities male aggressiveness is not observed, as this trait is frowned upon.

Castration in the immature male leads to excessive growth of the long bones, so that the height and the arm-span are increased. Testosterone facilitates fusion of the epiphysis (growing cap) of the long bones, and in the absence of the hormone the long bones are abnormally elongated. Administration of the hormone stimulates bone growth before the epiphyses fuse, and this accounts for the sudden spurt of growth at puberty. A characteristic feature of the adult eunuch (a person devoid of gonads) is that the arm-span exceeds the height. Fat is laid down over the buttocks and sometimes on the chest with the apparent formation of breasts, but there is no secreting tissue present. The skin is thin and the complexion sallow. An interesting feature is that the skin does not tan easily in ultra-violet light, possibly because of the low melanin production. If the accessory sex organs and secondary sex characters are present before castration there is little change, as once formed they do not readily atrophy, although growth of the hair on the face and body may decrease. The aggressiveness of the individual may increase or decrease, but there are also psychological factors to be considered. Castration produces serious mental problems for the afflicted individual. If sexual intercourse has been experienced the desire continues, but difficulty may be experienced in obtaining a satisfactory erection of the penis. Only by questioning the subject can any information be obtained about the success, or frequency, of sexual intercourse; obviously there is the desire to overestimate both their capacity and performance, but there is little doubt that the administration of testosterone will often improve the rigidity of the erect penis. Thus, observations on the castrate male are difficult, because of the profound effect it has on the mental approach of the individual.

The observed changes in the castrate boy and the restoration to full sexual development by the administration of testosterone show that the testes fulfil the criteria for an endocrine gland. It is not possible to describe the secondary sex characters of each class of animal and only a brief outline is given.

In all the sub-primate classes so far examined the male hormone is testosterone, except in the rat, where the hormone is the closely related androstenedione. The characteristic male feature, as in the higher primates, is the possession of the penis; the other accessory sex organs are essentially the same throughout the mammalian class (Fig. 4). An interesting difference is to be found in the secretion by an accessory sex organ, namely the prostates in man and rat; in the former the enzyme secreted is acid phosphatase while in the latter it is alkaline.

The secondary sex characters are wide and diverse, and have been considered elsewhere.[29] The growth of horns is of interest, as in some ruminants it is probably a sex characteristic, although the antler growth of some deer is directly controlled by adenohypophysial hormones. The final calcification is due to androgen secretion, and absence of the hormone leads to shedding of the antlers, whereas administration of the hormone prevents this.

Descent of the testicles

The mammals as a group characteristically carry the testes outside the body cavity in a sac, the scrotum. In this way the temperature of the testes is lower than that of the rest of the body, and this lower temperature is necessary for the normal production of spermatozoa: an increase in temperature, for example wrapping the scrotum in wool, will cut down spermatozoan production in these mammals. Some mammals, the whale, the elephant, the hyrax, etc., still retain the testes in the abdomen as in the sub-mammalian classes and in mammalian embryos. In those mammals possessing a scrotum the testes normally descend into it shortly before or about the time of birth, each one guided by a structure known as the gubernaculum testis. The detailed control of testicular descent is still uncertain, but it is probably brought about by the androgens produced by the foetal testes, possibly controlled by maternal gonadotrophins. If the testes have not descended shortly after birth, then in all probability they will not do so until sexual maturity, when there is increased androgen secretion. If the immature animal is given either androgens or gonadotrophins then the testes can be induced to descend.

In many seasonal-breeding mammals there is a phenomenon described as testicular descent at the breeding season, but in fact the process is rather one of a generalized increase in size of the sex organs including the scrotum. The testes have descended to the scrotum at birth, as in other mammals, but the structures remain small until the time of sexual activity and no obvious testes and scrotal sac are seen outside the breeding season.

BIRDS

John Hunter[37] noted both the sex differences and the marked seasonal changes in birds, but probably he was unaware that these changes were determined by the gonads.

The gonads of male foetuses may be ambisexual, the testis having a crust of cortical element, but this usually disappears after hatching. At an early stage in development the meta-nephros (the third and last embryonic kidney) takes over the excretory function, and the mesonephros (the second embryonic kidney), as in mammals, forms the vasa efferentia. After hatching, each sperm duct (vas deferens) becomes coiled, particularly at the lower end, and this acts as a storage organ (the glomus) for spermatozoa; the walls of the terminal part become thickened, forming the ejaculatory ducts. It is probable that all ancestral birds had a penis-like copulatory organ, but of the existing birds only the ostrich, duck and goose possess a penile structure.

At the breeding season the testis may increase some 300-fold in size owing to increased spermatogenesis and expansion of the tubules. This growth separates the interstitial tissue, and in the past has led to the mistaken assumption that this tissue decreases at the breeding season and hence could not be responsible for the secretion of androgens; it was believed that the male hormone was secreted by the tubules. However, androgens are still secreted by the testis in which the seminiferous tubules have been selectively destroyed by X-rays. It is therefore agreed that the interstitial cells of Leydig are the source of the androgen, which is probably testosterone. Two types of Leydig cells have been described, but it seems likely that they are the same cell at different stages of development. Probably the Sertoli cells are the source of oestrogen, as a tumour of these cells in the brown leghorn has been found to produce feminization of the male.

The accessory sex organs increase in size at seasonal breeding times, but the phallic organ of the duck does not show this seasonal change. It has been demonstrated that in the young duck the growth of the penis is due to the absence of female gonadal hormones, but the final enlargement at puberty is dependent upon adequate amounts of testosterone.

The terminal dilatation of the vas deferens is sometimes wrongly referred to as a seminal vesicle; it is really a seminal sac (or glomus), because in birds, unlike mammals, it acts as a storage organ. At the breeding season the sac becomes distended with spermatozoa; in some classes it may bulge into the cloaca, and may aid in intromission. Possibly this bulging allows the temperature in the sac to fall, increasing the viability of the spermatozoa, in which case it would function in a similar fashion to the scrotum of mammals. There is no homologue of the mammalian Cowper's gland, prostate and seminal vesicles.

The secondary sex characters are to be observed in the plumage, colour of the iris, in the shape and colour of the beak and in the voice. In the domestic fowl the head furnishings, namely the comb, wattles and ear lobes, are better developed in the male. Castration of the cock does not increase the true size of the bird, but it becomes fatter. A noticeable decrease in aggressiveness occurs in the castrate bird and the converse situation can be observed in the female bird given androgens; not only does the female become aggressive but she adopts a male courtship posture and may crow. An interesting action of androgen administration is to elevate the hen in the peck order (the more aggressive hens peck the less aggressive, forming various grades in the group). Androgen administration to the embryo, male or female, leads to the early development of a comb, and a few days after hatching the chicks may crow.

The plumage of birds and their control by hormones is a difficult subject that still remains to be clarified, as the effect of sex hormones varies in the different varieties of birds.[3] In general, it is possible to distinguish perennial and seasonal sex characters of the feathers; control of the former is mainly genetically determined and the latter is by hormones. Genetic control is widespread; it occurs where there are hen feathers in both sexes, or only the male has the cock plumage, or both sexes may have the cock feathers. The seasonal characters are controlled either by gonadal hormones, as in the ruff, or by adenohypophysial hormones, as in the orange and yellow weaver finches. In birds that indulge in a nuptial display, castration may lead to permanence of the cock plumage, but there is no information on the effects of this procedure when both sexes have a nuptial display. The plumage of the cock is the neuter form and the hen plumage is dependent on oestradiol. An ovary transplanted to the capon (castrated cock) leads to feminization of the plumage, but this is not permanent: possibly because of the growth of the medullary (testicular) part of the transplant. Interesting possibilities exist in the experimental field with those birds whose plumage is under the control of the pituitary gland, as this gland is in turn controlled by the hypothalamus, which is part of the central nervous system. The hormonal control of the plumage is probably phylogenetically the older type of control and, as evolution proceeds, the genetic type of control is becoming of greater prevalence.[43] The influence of the thyroid on feathering is considered in Chapter 5.

The colour of the bill in birds is produced by two varieties of melanin, brown and black, and three kinds of carotinoids, yellow, orange and red. In the house sparrows, African weaver finches and American indigo buntings the black colour of the beak at the breeding season is dependent upon the increased levels of testosterone, whereas in the common starling and the gull the beak becomes lighter in colour at the breeding season; this change is induced by the same hormone. The masked weaver is the only bird so far studied whose bill colour is determined by oestrogens. The paradise wydah shows seasonal changes of colour of the beak, but here the controlling agent appears to be LH. There is little doubt that the head furnishing of birds is principally controlled by androgens, but the growth of the spurs of cockerels is partly under the control of the thyroid gland.

There have been some claims that progesterone is present in male birds, and progesterone, or a progesterone-like substance, has been detected in the blood of cocks, but the methods used are far from specific. At present it would seem wise to assume that the sex hormones of male birds are the same as in other vertebrates, mainly testosterone and some oestrogen, but the function of the latter is still uncertain.

As migration may occur before sexual maturity, it cannot be influenced solely by gonadal activity. Apparently migration is controlled by the genetic constitution and its timing is determined by environmental changes. Alterations of metabolism that occur prior to migration (for example, laying down of body fat) and the actual stimulus to migrate are probably under the control of adenohypophysial hormones. Seasonal changes possibly induce some stimulation of the central nervous system which affects the hypothalamus, and the activity in this region determines the output of adenohypophysial hormones; an increased output of gonadotrophins will stimulate the gonads. The premigratory restlessness is partly under thyroid control.

REPTILES

All males possess an intromittent organ (except *Sphenodon*), but there is considerable variation in the size of this organ. The testes are inside the body cavity, often at different levels, and their structure is essentially the same as in mammals. Examination of the cloaca shows a sex dimorphism: the most obvious structure in the male is the penis which in lizards and snakes is paired, and as in other vertebrate classes its homologue in the female is the clitoris, a much smaller structure.

The reproductive ducts are basically similar in all classes below mammals. From the epididymis the vas deferens passes to open on to the genital papilla; spermatozoa pass from here along the urogenital sinus to the penis. Most reptiles are seasonal breeders and at the appropriate time the testes become active and the accessory sex organs enlarge.

In some reptiles, notably certain groups of lizards, there are well-marked sex differences in colour and body form. For example, in many agamid and iguanid lizards the male has appendages on the head and body such as gular pouches, dewlaps and erectile dorsal crests which may be poorly developed in the female. In lizards the males are usually more brilliant, but most snakes show little sex-colour difference. In boid snakes there are often vestigial spur-like hind limbs which may be larger in the males and are said to be used in courtship. In many lizards the distribution of the femoral pores differs in the two sexes; they may be absent in the females. In the long-snouted crocodiles known as the gavials there is in the male a swelling on the tip of the snout. While the function of this structure is unknown, it allows one to distinguish the sexes. Various species of chelonians show sex difference in such features as size, shape of the plastron, length of claws, etc.

In the kidneys of male lizards and snakes the uriniferous tubules of the preterminal segment (sexual segment) show considerable secretory activity which is controlled by the hormone of the testes. What may be regarded as seminal fluid is secreted by the sexual segment. This segment of the kidney is absent in females.

There is a period in the lives of many immature reptiles when both the medullary and cortical elements of the gonads are present in both sexes. Hermaphroditism has been reported in field studies of reptiles; and in birds some forms of bisexuality is also seen. In male reptiles, oviducts, portions of ovarian tissue and oocytes have been found in the testis; in the female, rudiments of the epididymis, vasa efferentia and vas deferens may be seen.

Castration has been carried out in a number of lizards and the effect is the same as in other vertebrates. In the sand lizard this procedure induces changes in the femoral glands and coloration of the body to that of a female; these, together with the accumulation of fat, give the general appearance of a female. There is little change in the copulatory organs, but there is shrinkage of the sexual segment of the kidney, epididymis and vas deferens. In castrated skinks (*Eumeces*) the hemipenis does not increase in size at the breeding season.

As injections of testosterone into the male embryos of terrapins (*Chrysemys marginata bellii*) are often lethal, the effects on the gonads are difficult to assess; in the female this hormone leads to intersexuality of the gonads, but there is little change in the accessory sex organs. This hormone administered to the pregnant garter snake, or directly injected into the amniotic cavity of the embryo, does not markedly affect the embryonic gonads. However, there is some stimulation of the medullary part of the gonads and of the Müllerian ducts. The observed difference between the two forms may be due to the fact that whereas the period of bisexuality of the gonads in the garter snakes is brief, in turtles it lasts several years. In newly hatched alligators testosterone injected into the male results in enlargement of the penis and, into the female, in hypertrophy of the oviducts, but the size of the clitoris is unaltered. In older animals the hormone induces enlargement of the penis in the male and the clitoris in the female. In the immature male lizard (*Sceloporus*) spermatogenesis is stimulated and the epididymis and vasa efferentia increase in size with this treatment. In the adult female (*Uromastix acanthinurus*), outside the period of sexual activity, the hormone induces development of the oviducal mucosa and sexual segment of the kidneys. Full sexual behaviour is brought about by injecting testosterone into the immature and castrate males, and into females both immature and fully grown. Androgens given to the male slider turtle results in enlargement of the penis, tail and digits of the claws.[44]

Oestrogens given to the male lizard embryo only slightly inhibit development of the medullary part of the testes, but markedly retard the development of the penis. In the immature male the hormone has a similar effect on the testes but the vas deferens and cloaca are stimulated.[44]

The male hormone in reptiles is testosterone and it is secreted by interstitial cells of the testes (cells of Leydig). Whether oestrogenic substances are secreted by the testes has yet to be clarified.

While it is accepted that the male hormone is testosterone, it is not known which cells of the testis are responsible for the secretion of this hormone. Under appropriate external conditions there is hypothalamic stimulation which induces increased gonadotrophic secretion from the adenohypophysis, stimulating spermatogenesis, and spermiation (expulsion of the spermatozoa to the exterior).

In general, castration in the immature animal leads to failure of the appearance of the secondary sex characters and development of accessory sex organs. This has been more extensively studied in the newts and salamanders, probably because the secondary sex characters are better developed in these. In the great crested newt (*Triturus cristatus*) these secondary sex characters are the nuptial coloration and dorsal crest; the accessory sex organs are the vas deferens, sexual segment of the kidney and the cloacal glands. The cloacae are different in the two sexes in the salamanders. In some male newts the toes enlarge in the breeding season. In some European newts the male is brightly coloured and there may be some form of display. At sexual maturity in male frogs (for example *Rana temporaria*) there is hypertrophy of the muscles of the forearms and thickening of the thumb-pads. If the immature animal is castrated these sex characters fail to appear, and this procedure may lead to their regression in the adult. Transplantation of the testis to the castrate restores the animal to normal. Administration of testosterone promotes the development of the sex characters in the immature male, but in the adult it is not always possible to induce the clasp reflex in the castrated frog with this hormone. It would appear that the development of the vocal pouch of the bull frog (*R. catesbiana*) is genetically determined.

In this class, naturally occurring hermaphroditism is fairly common. In toads the anterior ovarian lobe (Bidder's organ) is present, and after removal of the testes it develops into a functioning ovary. The vestigial Müllerian ducts are stimulated into full development and the transformation of a genetic male

53

to an apparent female is complete. Details of the secondary sex characters have been fully described in this class.[7]

FISHES

As the interstitial cells of Leydig appear at the time of maturity, it is suggested that this tissue may be the source of the male hormone, but not all classes of fish have these cells; instead they possess lobule boundary cells which may be the source of the male hormone. It is claimed that in the testis of the elasmobranch there are interstitial cells which are homologous with the Leydig cells. While it is accepted that the male possesses androgens, it is not known whether these are derived from a single hormone, testosterone. The male fish attains sexual maturity before the female and his life span is shorter; these two observations may be connected.

Fish are seasonal breeders and the secondary sex characters vary greatly in the different orders. The male may possess some form of gonopodium (a modified fin acting as a penis); the shape of the fin and colour of the body are often distinguishing features. The male Pacific salmon (*Oncorhynchus gorbuscha*) develops a secondary sex character at the end of a two-year life cycle which is a marked hump on the back due to growth of cartilage. The male reproductive ducts are basically similar to the higher poikilothermic vertebrates.

As with other vertebrates, spayed (castrated) immature fish fail to develop the secondary sex characters, and the animal fails to show the changes at the breeding season. Administration of testosterone to the castrate Poeciliidae leads to the development of the gonopodium, but the fin may not develop normally and the typical male pigment may not appear.

2 *The ovaries*

Throughout the Vertebrata the ovaries secrete oestradiol (or a closely related substance) which is a hormone mainly responsible for the development of the accessory sex organs and secondary sex characters. A second hormone, progesterone (Fig. 7), is present in the mammalian class and may be present in other vertebrates. This hormone probably acts synergistically with oestradiol to produce the changes described, and is also responsible for inducing the changes that occur following successful fertilization; in some classes of vertebrates, is believed to be responsible for the implantation of the fertilized ovum. Somewhat surprisingly, androgens are also secreted by the ovaries in many classes of vertebrates, but their precise role is unknown. A detailed review of the histological structure of the ovaries in the different vertebrate classes has been given.[3]

MAMMALS

Once again man is taken as the principal example of the primate class. At birth the ovaries contain ova and primordial follicles, and probably secrete oestradiol; nevertheless, as in the male, there is no further development of the sex characters until puberty, which usually occurs between ten and sixteen years. At this time the secondary sex characters appear. The laying down of fat at particular sites, the development of the breasts and the further specialized growth of the pelvis give rise to the typical contours of the female. While the growth of hair on the pubis, head, and in the armpits is probably not initiated by oestradiol (the oestrogenic hormone of the female), it is likely that this hormone promotes the growth once it has started. The accessory sex organs—namely, the uterus, the vagina and the external genitals—also begin to increase in size. It is suggested that the hormone mainly responsible for the development of the accessory sex organs and the secondary sex characters is oestradiol, a hormone which at this stage is probably derived from the interstitial cells of the ovary (Fig. 6). These cells possibly arise from follicles, which even in the foetus partially develop but then regress to form a small group of cells, and from primitive mesenchymal cells. Some degree of maturation of the follicle does occur in the absence of FSH.

At puberty in man and the higher primates, cyclical loss of blood from the vagina commences. The sequence of events which induces this change in man is as follows. An ovarian follicle fully

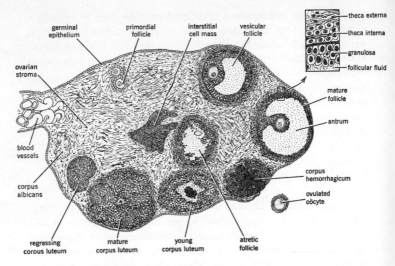

Fig. 6   Diagrammatic representation of the mammalian ovary. The development of the primordial follicle, and its subsequent formation into a corpus luteum, are shown. The regression of the latter and an atretic follicle are illustrated. Finally the layers of the mature follicle are drawn in the inset

(A modified reproduction from *A Textbook of Comparative Endocrinology* by Gorbman and Bern, by the courtesy of Messrs Wiley; this diagram is based in part on B. Patten and R. M. Eakin)

develops for the first time over a period of two weeks and then ruptures, releasing the ovum. The remaining cells of the follicle reform into a body known as a corpus luteum which lasts a similar time, provided pregnancy does not ensue. The follicle and the corpus luteum secrete oestradiol and progesterone respectively, but recently it has been shown that the corpus luteum may in addition secrete oestradiol. These hormones stimulate the lining of the uterus (endometrium) to proliferate. After a period of four weeks both hormones are absent, and the proliferated endometrium is desquamated and passes to the exterior with some blood (menstruation). Meanwhile another follicle in the ovary begins to ripen and secrete enough oestradiol to stimulate the endometrium once again and the process is repeated (menstrual cycle). In man the menstrual cycle which is dated from the onset of bleeding lasts about four weeks and the menstruation usually three to five days. The mechanism by which this cycle is regulated was discussed in the section on the adenohypophysial gonadotrophins. At puberty menstruation begins when the accessory and secondary sex factors have not yet reached full maturity and it may be that progesterone in addition to oestradiol is needed to achieve this state. Progesterone also reduces spontaneous uterine movements and the response to oxytocin.

Even long after puberty the breasts may show cyclical enlargement, reaching their maxima prior to menstruation and then regress to their original size, but these changes in volume are small. It is probable that this periodic alteration in the breast tissue is due to increased turgidity of the breast, secondary to increased vascularity, and is not due to a real increase of the glandular tissue. There are as well changes in the lining of the vagina during the menstrual cycle as evidenced by cornification of the superficial cells which are desquamated together with white blood cells at the time of ovulation.

Normally, the menstrual cycles continue until either the supply of ova in the ovaries is exhausted, or the ovaries become insensitive to the trophic hormones, and this usually occurs between the ages of forty and fifty years. The change is referred to as the menopause and marks the end of the reproductive period in the woman. At the menopause there may be mild mental changes, increased irritability and depression, but usually these symptoms cause no distress; very occasionally they are severe, and in addition there may be somatic alterations, for example vasomotor disturbances (flushing of the face) and osteoporosis (decreased calcium content of bone). Whether these changes are induced by a deficiency of oestradiol or by an excess of FSH, as the blood level of oestradiol has been markedly reduced, or are induced by psychological factors (the mental trauma of knowing that the reproductive period is at an end), is difficult to decide; probably both hormonal and psychological factors play a part. Certainly the administration of oestradiol in amounts comparable to that normally secreted by the ovaries does often result in a marked improvement of the menopausal symptoms. If the menopause is induced at a young age by removal or destruction of the ovaries, these symptoms may be very severe.

Removal of the ovaries before puberty leads to failure of both the development of the secondary sex characters and the further development of the accessory sex organs, that is the uterus, the vagina and external genitals. Often there is a stunting of growth, but occasionally the typical stature of a eunuch may be observed. Administration of an oestrogen to growing females will at first accelerate growth, which then ceases, as the hormone after stimulation causes fusion of the epiphyses to the shaft of the long bones (cf. testosterone in the male). Ovariectomy in the adult woman induces little change in the secondary sex characters, but excess fat may be deposited in the breasts, and the accessory sex organs may shrink after a while.

Oestradiol alone will induce the growth of the accessory sex organs and secondary sex characters in the spayed child and withdrawal of this hormone results in vaginal bleeding, but the changes seen in the endometrium are not comparable to those normally observed just before menstruation. To induce the normal pre-menstrual state in the endometrium, it is necessary to administer both oestradiol and progesterone. Usually oestradiol, or its equivalent, is given for two weeks and towards the end of this period progesterone is administered for a similar time. A few days after cessation of therapy a menstrual flow occurs. During the menstrual cycle, in the normal adult woman, it would appear that about 0·015 mg of oestradiol are produced daily during follicular development, and about 20 mg per day of progesterone during the luteal phase (the period in which the corpus luteum is secreting).

Estimations of the hormone in the urine have shown that the peak excretion of oestradiol and its metabolic products, oestrone and oestriol, occurs about the fourteenth day of the menstrual cycle. The peak for excretion of the derivatives of progesterone occurs about a week before menstruation, and at this time the excretion of oestrogens rises again. These levels are at their lowest just prior to menstruation. It must be emphasized that the methods of estimating the hormones in the urine are subject to large errors.

At the commencement of sexual life the cycles may be anovulatory, that is the ovum is not expelled, but the follicle having almost achieved maturity degenerates and no corpus luteum develops. There is bleeding due to the fall of the oestradiol blood level. Histological examination of the endometrium reveals that the stimulation has been incomplete, because the changes induced by progesterone are absent. An observation of value is that at ovulation there is usually a rise of body temperature and thus it is possible to date this event.

There are two other points of interest with regard to oestradiol. First, there are synthetic materials whose formulae are quite different to oestradiol, but which have oestrogenic action. Secondly, in the experimental animal oestrogenic substances have been shown to be carcinogenic agents; that is, they are an important factor in initiating, or promoting, the growth of a cancer. The importance of this in man remains to be elucidated.

In mammals below the higher primates, the ovaries are responsible for the development of the female accessory and secondary sex factors and the oestradiol is probably the hormone mainly responsible for these changes. Further, this hormone induces 'heat' or oestrus. The vagina of the rat is very sensitive to oestradiol which induces cornification. Thus examination of the vaginal cells will establish whether the rat is in oestrus (superficial vaginal cells can be obtained by merely washing out the vagina). The lining of the vagina of the rabbit appears to be insensitive to oestradiol. Mammals may fall anywhere between these two extremes, and man is about halfway.

Oestrus may occur many times in a year (polyoestrus), as in the rat and mouse (both have short oestrus cycles), or only once a year (monoestrus) as in the silver fox. The short-cycle rodents are spontaneous ovulators, while the cat, ferret and rabbit are induced ovulators, usually requiring coitus in order to ovulate. In the former group there is no functional luteal phase, but in the ungulates and the dog the luteal phase is prolonged and significant quantities of progesterone are secreted. The short-cycle spontaneous ovulators must have an appropriate neurogenic stimulus (coitus) to induce the release of LTH which initiates hormonal secretion by the corpus luteum. It appears that the seasonal activity, commonly seen in these mammals, is induced by changes in the gonads which are controlled by the trophic hormones of the adenohypophysis, and this in turn is under the domination of the hypothalamus. This seasonal breeding is so formulated that the young are born at a propitious time. Details on seasonal cycles and pseudopregnancy in the lower mammals have been discussed.[29]

BIRDS

The ovaries are the source of oestrogens (probably oestradiol), androgens and possibly progesterone, or a progesterone-like material. In most avian groups on the left side there is an ovary and a fully developed oviduct, while on the right there is an ovatestis; in the birds of prey both sides may have an ovary, and this may occasionally occur in the non-raptorial series.

Viviparity does not occur in birds and therefore the female accessory sex organs are relatively simple, when compared to mammals. The relationship of the oviduct to the ovary is fairly constant throughout all classes of birds. The oviducts are long, ciliated and very distensible, and at the appropriate time the duct wall pushes the egg towards the exterior by peristaltic movements. Fertilization usually occurs before the egg has reached the glandular-secreting part of the duct. The viability of the spermatozoa inside the duct is probably several days.

Thickened peritoneal epithelium alongside the mesonephric ducts in the female embryo form the oviducts. On the left the duct continues to increase in size after differentiation of the gonads. The seasonal hypertrophy of the oviducts and the secretion of albumin by the glandular portion are under the control of oestrogens and possibly progesterone. The shell gland which secretes the calcareous material does not store calcium; this is in the medullary bone which has been laid down earlier, under the influence of oestrogen.

In many classes of birds the vasa deferentia and seminal sacs are present in the females and during the breeding season the ducts enlarge, the lumens becoming filled with secretory material. This observed enlargement and secretory activity is good evidence of androgen secretion.

As in mammals, not all the follicles ripen and produce ova. The fully developed follicle is very vascular and contains a fluid which is a rich source of oestrogen. After rupture no permanent corpus luteum forms, but fibroblasts infiltrate the area. The stroma of the ovary contains secretory cells which probably arise, as in mammals, from atretic follicles and from primitive mesenchymal cells.

There is still considerable doubt whether progesterone is secreted by the ovaries. In hens there is evidence that administered progesterone may induce LH secretion and hence ovulation. It may be that in this class the classical negative feedback of ovarian hormones on the secretions of the adenohypophysis, observed in mammals, is not applicable.

The secondary sex characters have been discussed when dealing with the male, and only a brief outline of the action of oestrogen in birds will be given. In the domestic fowl, turkey and pheasant ovariectomy results in the animal assuming the male plumage. Transplants of the ovary to the capon result in a female type of feathering. If the plumage is dependent on oestrogens, the characteristic growth of the feathers in different parts of the body is believed to be due to local alterations of sensitivity to this hormone.

Oestrogens stimulate nest-building activity. They are in part responsible for the behavioural characters at breeding time and they stop broodiness. Administration of oestrogens to cockerels, or transplants of ovaries into capons, lead to female behaviour. Generally, oestrogen administration to the male leads to suppression of the male type of plumage, but sensitivity varies from one class to another. Gynandromorphism may be seen in which one half of the animal has male feathering and the other female. This may be due to the sex chromosomes being different on the two sides of the body. In birds oestrogen has an additional action not seen in other vertebrates in that it stimulates metabolism and the blood calcium may rise even in the absence of the parathyroids (Chapter 6).

Removal of the left ovary is usually difficult as the ovary is diffuse, but when this is affected by disease and destroyed the right gonad becomes a testis which results in the bird developing male characters; sufficient ovarian tissue sometimes remains on the diseased side allowing the bird to lay eggs, and this results in the interesting paradox referred to as the 'laying cock'. If an ovary is transplanted to an immature male, the bird is feminized.

The behaviour of birds is influenced by hormones. Progesterone may be responsible for broodiness and the behavioural characteristics seen at incubation. At particular periods many birds exhibit male behaviour and it has been claimed that this is due to androgen secretion by the ovaries; the effects of oestrogens have been discussed. Thus the sex hormones may be responsible for many of the characteristic changes during and after the breeding season, but they cannot account for all the alterations. Genetic factors, together with visual impressions during the early part of life, make a significant contribution to behaviour.

REPTILES

The ovaries are hollow structures lying in the abdominal cavity and may be at different levels. The oviducts remain separate and fertilization occurs in the upper part. Apparently spermatozoa may remain viable for several months in the oviducts. Most reptiles lay eggs, but many lizards and snakes are viviparous. The term ovoviviparity, in preference to viviparity, is sometimes applied to the birth of live young in reptiles, as it is claimed that the nutrition of the foetus in this class depends on the egg-yolk and not on the placenta. In some classes the embryo is maintained by placental nutrition, and thus, for simplicity, viviparity may be applied to the birth of live young in reptiles.

Comparison of the secondary sex characters has been considered in the section on male reptiles. Ovariectomy results in marked atrophy of the oviducts and urogenital sinus. If the operation is carried out in the breeding season, the animal ceases to show the characteristic behaviour changes which occur at this period. This procedure may increase the aggressiveness, and it is possible that this feature, shown by the male, may be due to lack of ovarian hormones. Ovariectomy in pregnant viviparous reptiles at any stage of pregnancy does not usually affect the development of the eggs or cause their premature expulsion; that is, embryonic development as such is not affected. However, this procedure generally induces disturbances of parturition, either premature or delayed birth, often resulting in death of the embryos.

Oestrogens, like testosterone, are toxic in the cold-blooded vertebrates and this makes the interpretation of the results difficult. In the reptilian embryo both the medullary and cortical regions of the gonads and the Müllerian ducts are stimulated by the administration of oestrogens; similar effects are produced in the immature animal. This hormone will also induce the early appearance of the secondary sex characters and cornification of the cloaca. While oestrogens stimulate the cortical and medullary parts of the gonads in the female, they have a small retarding action on the medulla of the male gonad.[44]

From a study of the effects of injection of various oestrogens it appears likely that oestradiol, or a similar substance, is the hormone secreted by the ovaries. The sources of the hormone are the interstitial cells and probably the developing follicles in the ovaries. Although corpora lutea may appear in the ovaries of reptiles, it is unlikely that progesterone is secreted. In evolution it would seem that the corpora lutea appeared before developing a true endocrine function.

AMPHIBIANS

It is the male which usually possesses the characteristic features that allow sexual differentiation to be made; in this respect the amphibians are similar to the reptiles. Further, the ovaries are hollow, but there is more evidence of medullary activity in this class.

As oestradiol injections do not restore some of the female characters of ovariectomized amphibians, it is believed that oestradiol is not the hormone secreted by the ovaries, but that it is probably closely related to this substance. The main accessory sex organs are the oviducts, and removal of the ovaries results in degeneration of these with loss of the mating reflex. It is possible to feminize a genetic male at an early age by removing the testes and replacing them by an ovary. If a male and a female salamander are joined by parabiosis (this allows the blood of the two animals to mix), a blood-borne substance from the male will lead to complete involution of the ovaries. The same experimental procedure in frog tadpoles also partially inhibits the ovaries, but the effect decreases as the distance from the ovaries to the testes increases, unlike the effect seen in the salamander which is independent of the distance; if the female tadpole is bigger than the male, the reverse occurs and the testes are affected. It is suggested that in tadpoles the gonads produce a material which diffuses locally and affects the gonads of the other sex.

Mammalian growth hormone or LH will induce ovulation of the isolated ovaries. There is evidence that adrenal steroids and progesterone may also promote ovulation in the absence of the pituitary gland and oestrogens inhibit this action. It appears likely that under normal conditions pituitary hormones acting synergistically with adrenal cortical hormones induce ovulation.

FISHES

As in the other poikilothermic vertebrates, the ovaries are hollow. There are only a few secondary sex characters in the female, for example the growth of specific fins, colour, and in some the presence of a genital tubercle. It is of interest that the male will court ovariectomized females, even in the presence of normal ones. Nevertheless, removal of the ovaries does markedly disturb the sex behaviour.

It would appear that oestradiol is not the hormone secreted by the ovaries as on administration it does not restore the colour of spayed fish and the restoration of the social hierarchy is only achieved with testosterone; further, testosterone is more effective in enlarging the genital tubercle than oestradiol. This has led to some doubt as to whether the ovaries secrete any oestrogens, but chromatographic studies have shown the presence of oestriol and small quantities of oestradiol (Fig. 7): in addition, progesterone may be present. The indefinite results obtained with the administration of oestradiol in spayed fish could be due to a seasonal variation in the tissue response to this hormone.

It would seem likely that oestrogens are secreted by the follicles of the ovaries. The luteinized granulosa cells are apparently responsible for the secretion, or resorption of the egg-yolk in those fish which lay eggs. There is some evidence that in the viviparous species of elasmobranchs the luteinized granulosa cells may secrete progesterone.

While cyclical changes in the ovaries are responsible for seasonal breeding, their part in the migration of fish is still uncertain.

Summary

The genetic constitution of the animal determines whether ovaries or testes develop from the primitive gonads. Once differentiated, it is believed that the appropriate gonadal hormones are responsible for the further development of the accessory sex organs; these may be conveniently defined as those structures which aid in the transmission of gametes, and at the same time add some constituents which are necessary both for their viability and for successful fertilization. Whether the embryonic hormones of the gonads are identical with those in the adult has not yet been established. Thus the function of the gonads is a dual one—formation of gametes and secretion of hormones.

In the main, the hormone secreted by the vertebrate testis is testosterone; the rat is given as an exception in the mammalian class, as here the hormone appears to be androstenedione. There is some doubt as to the site of origin of testosterone in amphibians, and some fish do not possess the interstitial cells of Leydig, but in all other classes of vertebrates these cells secrete the hormone. Somewhat surprisingly, in many vertebrates oestrogens are secreted by the testis, probably by the Sertoli cells, but whether this hormone has a physiological action is still in doubt. This hormone may be an incidental by-product, and its presence is only apparent in man in pathological conditions.

Besides the genetic and gonadal (primary) there are the secondary sex characters. These are the external characters which enable the sexes to be differentiated. The separation of

C

these characters from accessory sex organs may be somewhat false, but it is nevertheless convenient. These features have been considered in some detail in man, but in the other mammals only some aspects have been discussed. In birds the important sex characters, namely the plumage and head furnishings, have been dealt with in a condensed form, because the subject is complex and ill understood. While migration is usually associated with gonadal activity, gonadal hormones are not the causal factor. In the poikilothermic vertebrates some sex characters have been discussed, but of the very many only a few have been studied to any degree. In all classes below mammals some degree of ambi-sexuality is common.

In all vertebrates testosterone, or a closely related substance, is probably responsible for the post-embryonic development of the accessory sex organs, the acquisition of the secondary sex characters and the sex drive; the latter may not be entirely hormonally determined in man. The changes induced by castra-tion in the adult animal may not always be dramatic, and it is far simpler to establish that the testis is an endocrine gland in the immature. Castration at an early age results in a failure of devel-opment of the discussed sex organs and characters, but these will develop normally if testosterone is administered. In adult man castration may apparently induce very little change. Even the sex drive may continue unabated, but intromission is often difficult. It would seem that man, once fully developed, is almost freed from the necessity of gonadal hormones.

The ovaries in the vertebrate class secrete oestradiol or a closely related substance. This is the main feminizing hormone, which is responsible for the further development of the accessory sex organs and for the development of the secondary sex characters. In man and the higher primates a second hormone, progesterone, is probably needed for full sexual maturity. This hormone also causes the endometrium to thicken, the glands to secrete, and the blood vessels to become coiled; that is the lining is fully prepared to receive the fertilized ovum. This action of pro-gesterone is common throughout the mammalian class, but in some, mice, rats and hamsters, there is no functioning corpus luteum unless the nervous stimulus of coitus is applied.

The cells which secrete oestradiol, or an oestrogen, are the interstitial cells of the ovary and the thecal cells of the developing follicle: progesterone is secreted by the granulosa cells of the corpus luteum.

While in domesticated lower mammals the male may be sexually active at all times, the female has cycles of 'heat' (oestrus) when blood may be lost from the vagina. This does not correspond to the menses of the higher primates, as the oestrus period occurs at the time of ovulation. In women there may be a loss of blood from the vagina between the menses, and when this occurs it is comparable to the oestrus of the lower mammals. Under natural conditions the breeding habits of the mammals, and indeed of other vertebrates, are such that the young are born at a propitious time—even the male is a seasonal breeder. It is believed that the external environment in some way monitors the inherent clock-like mechanism of the hypothalamus, which determines the output of adenohypophysial hormones, and these in turn control the gonads. Man, the higher primates, and to some degree the domesticated male mammals, may breed at any time of the year, and are apparently free from the effects of the external environment.

In the females of mammals below primates, birds, and the poikilothermic vertebrates, the sex drive and the characteristic behaviour involved in the successful rearing of the young appear to be in some degree controlled by hormones. Indeed, some would go further and suggest that they are entirely responsible for these complex changes. In contrast, women appear to be less dependent on hormones for their sex drive, but are more susceptible to their influences than men. Whereas in the male no known hormone increases the libido, it is claimed that androgens are effective in this respect in women.

Viviparity does occur outside the mammalian class, in reptiles, some fish and a few amphibians. As there are so few facts known about this process in these classes, it has only received brief consideration. Here viviparity is probably not dependent on progesterone, as there is no definite evidence that this hormone exists in any class below mammals.

In man, and in many classes of vertebrates, the ovaries secrete androgens, which are probably derived from the interstitial cells. The role of androgens in the female is comparable to that of oestrogens in the male. However, in the case of the female, certain claims have been made as to their function. They are important protein anabolizers, and on much less certain grounds it has been suggested that they may be responsible for the sex drive of the female.

4

The adrenal glands

IN MAMMALS the adrenal is clearly organized into two parts, an outer cortex and an inner medulla, and functionally they are two separate endocrine glands. The adrenal cortex develops in the foetus from the coelomic epithelium which also gives rise to the gonads. The medulla (chromaffin tissue) arises from those cells which subsequently form the sympathetic ganglia. The anatomical organization of the medulla and the cortex seen in mammals has led to a number of interesting speculations why these two glands should be in such intimate association. One possible explanation is that adrenaline constricts the medullary arteries and this would result in a richer blood flow to the cortex. Another is that adrenaline directly stimulates the biosynthesis of the steroid hormones.

In vertebrates below mammals the medulla is not usually a compact tissue in the centre of the adrenal and is preferably referred to as chromaffin tissue. The term adrenal cortex can be retained for all the vertebrate classes, but in the fish in view of the anatomical position the synonym interrenal may be preferred.

1 Adrenal cortex

MAMMALS

This gland in mammals is discussed under three separate headings: Eutherian (foetus nurtured by a placenta), Metatherian (the young are born in a primitive state and subsequently develop in the pouch of the mother) and Prototherian (egg-layers). The

Metatherian and Prototherian will be only briefly discussed. The reader should refer for detailed discussion of the adrenal cortex in the vertebrates to the concise and excellent review by Chester Jones.[6]

(A) EUTHERIAN

It is generally agreed that the adrenal cortex is essential for life, but in some classes (for example the rat) it has been claimed that the adrenalectomized animal will sometimes survive if given extra salt. It is likely, however, that on such occasions the adrenalectomy is incomplete, in that accessory cortical tissue may be present, and this would account for the apparent discrepancy.

Histology. The cortex has a characteristic appearance and three zones can usually be distinguished. The outermost layer is the zona glomerulosa, so called because the cells are arranged in small spheres, and this zone is relatively thin. In the next region the cells are arranged in columns and this is referred to as the zona fasciculata. The cells in the innermost layer are in the form of a reticulum—the zona reticularis. Not all mammals have these three distinct zones and it is doubtful if the monkey has a zona glomerulosa.

The cortical cells have a high content of lipid (a fatty material) and, with standard methods of embedding in wax and subsequently dissolving the wax with a fat solvent, the lipid in the cells is also removed. Therefore, when wax sections of the tissue are examined microscopically, the cytoplasm of the cells has clear areas and this imparts to the cells their characteristic appearance. The cells also contain large quantities of ascorbic acid. Only recently has the functional significance of the various zones been appreciated. The zona glomerulosa secretes mineralocorticoid, while the inner zones secrete the glucocorticoid hormones.

Active principles. The division of adrenal cortical hormones into glucocorticoids and mineralocorticoids is a convenient one, but it must be realized that there is some overlapping of their activities. Whether this classification can be applied to vertebrates outside the mammalian class is still uncertain. The adrenal cortex is a very active gland, and, while the rates of synthesis and secretion are high, the quantity of hormones stored is small. Under these circumstances any attempt to extract the hormones from the cortex results in many intermediary metabolic precursors of the hormone being isolated, and these precursors may have specific physiological actions. This was responsible for the erroneous idea that the adrenal cortex secreted over twenty hormones. It is likely that there are only two main hormones secreted, a mineralo-corticoid and a glucocorticoid, so named by virtue of their action and structure.

In 1937 deoxycorticosterone (DOC)[61] was synthesized and it was suggested that this substance might be the mineralocorticoid hormone of the adrenal cortex, as it would correct both the sodium and potassium imbalance of adrenalectomized mammals. However, there was doubt whether this was the hormone, since only minute quantities could be extracted from the cortex.

In 1950 cortisone became available on a commercial scale and it was found that this hormone, when given to patients with adrenal deficiency, would correct the impaired carbohydrate metabolism. It was assumed that cortisone was the glucocorticoid hormone. It was now possible to treat adequately these patients, or adrenalectomized animals, using DOC and cortisone.

In 1952 a crystalline steroid[58] was isolated from adrenal extracts which was initially called electrocortin, because of its profound effect on the concentration of sodium and potassium in the body. Subsequently it was established that this was the mineralocorticoid hormone of the cortex and it was renamed aldosterone. Aldosterone is some thirty times more potent than DOC and it has some glucocorticoid activity, weight for weight about one-third of that of cortisone. As to the glucocorticoid, this varies in different mammals: in man the hormone is 17-hydroxycorticosterone (cortisol) with possible small quantities of 17-hydroxy 11-dehydrocorticosterone (cortisone); in the rabbit the main hormone is corticosterone (Fig. 7). The glucocorticoids promote gluconeogenesis, which, briefly, convert proteins and fats into glucose. This process is important in maintaining the blood glucose, as the only other source of glucose is glycogen and the body stores of this substance are relatively low.

Control. Hypophysectomy results in shrinkage mainly of the zona fasciculata and reticularis, and the blood glucose falls.

Injections of ACTH not only restore the normal histological appearance, but the defect of impaired gluconeogenesis is also corrected. As the administration of an excess of glucocorticoids to an intact animal induces the same histological changes in the adrenal cortex as hypophysectomy, it is assumed that the output of ACTH has been suppressed. Thus it is believed that there is a reciprocal relationship between ACTH and glucocorticoids. Normally the correct quantity of ACTH is secreted to produce an adequate amount of glucocorticoids and this hormone acts on the adenohypophysis directly, or indirectly via the hypothalamus, preventing an excess secretion of ACTH. This self-balancing mechanism is a stable one and, if glucocorticoids are given, signs of an excess are only seen when the quantity administered exceeds the amount normally secreted.

It is likely that ACTH does in part control aldosterone secretion, as following hypophysectomy there are small disturbances of sodium and potassium balance, but there are other mechanisms. It has been suggested that changes of intravascular volume alter the activity of afferent nerves which are in the walls of arterial blood vessels. These nerves run to the hypothalamus and their activity determines the rate of secretion of a putative hormone (adrenoglomerulotrophin) which in turn controls the output of aldosterone: the pineal may be the source of adrenoglomerulotrophin (Chapter 10).

Possibly the blood level of angiotensin is the factor controlling aldosterone secretion. Angiotensin is formed from the inactive angiotensinogen in the blood by the action of the enzyme renin, which is secreted by the kidney when its blood flow is reduced, as would occur following a fall of blood volume. It is true that under normal conditions plasma volume is maintained within narrow limits and the maintenance of this volume is essential for normal function, but further work is necessary to establish which mechanism, if any, is responsible.

There appears to be another mechanism which also controls mineralocorticoid hormone secretion, namely the blood potassium level. A rise or fall of blood potassium stimulates, or inhibits, the secretion of the hormone respectively. An increase in the level of mineralocorticoid hormone will enhance the renal

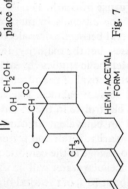

CORTICOSTERONE

Deoxycorticosterone is equivalent to Corticosterone minus HO— group at 11 position

Cortisol is equivalent to Corticosterone plus —OH group at 17 position

Cortisone is equivalent to Corticosterone plus —OH group at 17 position and =O in place of HO— group at 11 position

ALDOSTERONE

ALDEHYDE FORM

HEMI-ACETAL FORM

PROGESTERONE

Testosterone is equivalent to Progesterone plus —OH group at 17 position in place of COCH₃

OESTRADIOL

Oestrone is equivalent to Oestradiol plus =O in place of —OH group at 17 position

Oestriol is equivalent to Oestradiol plus —OH group at 16 position

Fig. 7 The structural formulae of the steroid hormones. In solution aldosterone is mainly present as the hemi-acetal form

excretion of potassium. Thus this type of control would regulate the blood potassium level within narrow limits.

It must be emphasized that at present the control of aldosterone secretion is still uncertain.

Function. Man has been selected as the principal example of the Eutherians. Addison (1868)[8] by careful clinico-pathological observations concluded that the adrenals were essential for life. In addition, he observed that before the patients with degenerated adrenals died they showed characteristic clinical features: weakness, impaired action of the heart, pigmentation of the skin and episodes of diarrhoea and vomiting. In acknowledgment of this great work adrenal deficiency in man is called Addison's disease.

A few years later it was shown that adrenalectomy in lower mammals was invariably fatal, but, as post-operative infections commonly occurred, it was possible that this complication was the cause of death. During the years 1920–30 it was established that the adrenals in mammals were essential for life: the time interval between adrenalectomy and death varied in the different classes, but the majority died within a few days.

Metabolic studies revealed that destruction by disease or surgical removal of the adrenals produced profound effects on water and sodium balance. Excess sodium was excreted and a fall of this electrolyte in the blood depressed the output of vasopressin and an equivalent amount of water was lost to maintain iso-osmolarity. If salt and water are lost in equivalent amounts there is no change in the osmotic pressure of the extracellular fluid and intracellular water will be unaffected. This is of great importance as about 70% of the total body water is in the cells. If water alone is lost, however, the osmotic pressure of the extracellular fluid rises and water will leave the cells until the iso-osmotic equilibrium is restored. Hence a water deficit is borne by the whole fluid system, whereas a loss of both salt and water affects only the extracellular volume which includes the blood volume. Enhanced excretion of salt and water will lower the blood volume and the cardiac output will fall; this results in an impaired circulation. Kidney function is depressed, as this is partially dependent on blood pressure, and this impairment is reflected by a rise of the blood urea (a breakdown product of proteins).

The iso-osmolarity of the blood is maintained until the blood volume falls to a low level, when water is retained, apparently in an endeavour to maintain this volume; at this juncture the plasma sodium begins to fall. It is at this stage that the animal is likely to die. The fall in blood volume in patients with Addison's disease is responsible for the low blood pressure which Addison recognized as feebleness of the heart's action. Loss of the fluid component of blood results in a rise of the concentration of the cellular part, and the blood becomes more viscous: the red cell count rises and the oxygen-carrying power of the blood increases.

The adrenal cortical hormones control sodium excretion by promoting their re-absorption, partly in exchange for intra-cellular potassium in the distal portion of the tubules of the kidney. If there is a deficiency of aldosterone, excessive amounts of sodium are excreted depleting the organism of this ion and there is a rise of plasma potassium, which could be due to three separate mechanisms. First, less potassium is exchanged for sodium in the kidney tubules and, secondly, potassium will leak out of the cells of the body which have a high concentration of this ion. Thirdly, dehydration by itself may be responsible for potassium leaving the intracellular compartment. Whether these factors operate singly or together is not known, but a rise of plasma potassium is toxic and will induce muscular and cardiac weakness; if the level rises very high, death will occur.

It has also been noted that in the absence of the adrenals the blood glucose will fall, owing to impaired gluconeogenesis. If the blood glucose is sufficiently depressed there is disturbed mental function and eventually death of the animal.

When in 1895 a vasoconstrictor substance was isolated from the adrenal medulla[51] it was suggested that the fall in blood pressure observed in patients with Addison's disease was due to the absence of this substance. Subsequent investigations demon-strated, however, that all the clinical features of adrenalectomy could be induced by removal of the cortical tissue.

In patients with Addison's disease there is excess pigmentation of the skin and it had been suggested that this was due to an increase in the amount of available tyrosine (an amino acid).

Tyrosine not only forms the basis of the molecular structure of adrenaline, but is also necessary for the formation of melanin. If adrenaline synthesis ceased, then there would be a surfeit of tyrosine for conversion into melanin and hence pigmentation would increase. This view is no longer held and it is believed that the high blood level of ACTH (induced by the absence of the inhibiting action of glucocorticoids) is responsible. This aspect is discussed further in Chapter 10 in the section on pigmentation. It is of interest that adrenal deficiency in the lower mammals does not result in increased pigmentation.

Secretion of gonadal hormones

There is some evidence that the adrenal cortex secretes gonadal hormones—oestrogens, androgens and progesterone, or progesterone-like substances. The evidence in favour of this is indirect, and briefly is based on the following observations. First, the cells that give rise to the adrenal cortex are closely related to those that eventually form the gonads. Secondly, it is suggested that the continued sex drive and cyclical changes in vaginal cytology (Chapter 3), which occur in some mammals after spaying, are due to adrenal cortical secretion: in many laboratory animals there is enlargement of the adrenals after castration. Thirdly, reference to Fig. 7 reveals that the structural formulae of gonadal and adrenal cortical hormones are very similar; and it would appear likely that there may be some overlapping of their physiological action (progesterone administration will maintain the life of the adrenalectomized animal). Fourthly, tumours of the adrenal cortex in man may profoundly affect sexual differentiation. This is discussed in detail in the next section. As progesterone appears to be an intermediary metabolite in the formation of adrenal cortical hormones, it is difficult to decide whether it is a true hormone of this gland.

Effects of adrenal cortical tumours in man

1. *Sex hormone excess.* Some types of adrenal cortical tumours, when they arise in the female embryo, induce masculinization of the genital tract, and at birth there may be great difficulty in determining the sex of the individual. When this condition occurs

in the adult female, only the clitoris (the homologue of the penis) enlarges, as the remainder of the genitals are fully developed; there is, as well, increased hairiness of the body and face. In the young boy similar tumours produce precocious sexual development, and the sex organs and drive are that of an adult. It is interesting that these tumours of the adrenal cortex apparently only secrete androgens.

2. *Glucocorticoid excess*. An excess of this hormone as expected induces increased gluconeogenesis, but mainly protein is catabolized. Not only is the muscle mass reduced, but also the protein matrix of the bone, and this results in weakness and decalcification respectively. The blood glucose rises and synthesis of fat increases (Chapter 7), resulting in an excess being deposited, usually in certain typical sites. The glycogen content of the liver increases. Loss of protein from the skin which reduces its elasticity and the subdermal deposition of fat are probably partially responsible for the characteristic purple striae. For reasons which still remain obscure, the red cell count increases. As this hormone possesses some intrinsic mineralocorticoid activity there will be electrolyte disturbances, which are described in the next section.

3. *Mineralocorticoid excess*. This leads to excess salt and water retention with some expansion of the plasma volume. Of greater importance is the fall of blood potassium, due to enhanced excretion of this electrolyte by the kidney, which results in muscular weakness.

It is possible to find any combination of these excesses and it has been reported that an excess of one hormone may be associated with a deficiency of another. It must be emphasized that there may be adrenal cortical tumours without hormonal disturbance.

The adrenal cortex of the newborn infant

This differs from the adult in that the glands are large, about one-third the size of the kidneys, and consist of a mass of primitive gonadal cells; the typical adult type of cortical cells are present, but only at the periphery. After birth these peripheral cells increase in number and slowly grow in to replace the primitive cells. This raises the problem whether the newborn infant secretes adult adrenal cortical hormones, or whether the hormones are mainly gonadal. It is possible that newborn infants are relatively deficient of cortical hormones and this might account for their susceptibility to infection.

The X zone

The adrenal of the mouse is unusual in that it possesses a specialized area, between the medulla and the cortex, referred to as the X zone. These cells have different staining properties to the cortical cells, and are under the control of the gonadotrophins. This zone is first recognizable some fourteen days after birth, and it, together with the adrenal cortex, increases in size. In the male this zone degenerates at puberty due to the action of androgens. In the unmated female at puberty the zone may occupy 50% of the adrenal cortex, and in middle life it slowly degenerates. If pregnancy occurs, these cells rapidly disintegrate between the seventh and twelfth days. Whether the X zone secretes any hormones remains to be established. An X zone has been reported in other mammals, namely the cat, rabbit and the female golden hamster.

Adrenal size and population

It has been found that in small mammals adrenal size and population are related; the more dense the population the greater the adrenal size. It has been suggested that the enlarged adrenals secrete androgens which inhibit the output of gonadotrophins. This would lead to a failure of reproduction and a fall in the population. Thus the size of any confined group would be self-limiting.

Cortisone in clinical medicine

In 1949[34] it was reported that cortisone would reduce the inflammation and pain in patients with rheumatoid arthritis—a common and crippling disease. Many theories were presented to account for this observation, but the one proposed by Selye[57] found the greatest acceptance. He suggested that adrenal cortical hormones were essential in the adaptation of the organism to sustained injurious influences (this includes infection); 'stress' was the word used to define this stimulus. The responses of the animal to stress were grouped together under the term 'general adaptation syndrome'. This was said to consist of three phases—an 'alarm reaction' which is seen at the commencement and corresponds to the condition of shock and recovery; the 'stage of adaptation', when the animal becomes resistant to the stress, is associated with adrenal cortical hypertrophy and possibly with an increased output of cortical hormones; finally in the 'stage of exhaustion' the adrenal cortex fails and the animal dies. It was suggested that the general responses to all stressful conditions were similar. During the stage of adaptation there may be an imbalance of output of cortical hormones, possibly an excess of mineralocorticoid. Selye had shown that this hormone in the rat, under rather special conditions, would induce pathological changes similar to those seen in diseases of man (rheumatoid arthritis was one). When this imbalance occurred, reference was made to 'diseases of adaptation'. From this hypothesis it was possible to predict that glucocorticoids might be of benefit in these diseases of man, but the evidence against this concept is overwhelming and it must be discarded.

It would seem that cortisone (or cortisol) acts in some way to suppress inflammatory changes and it also inhibits fibroblast formation. Whenever tissues are destroyed, fibroblasts infiltrate and the subsequent scarring may lead to troublesome deformities. This inhibitory action of cortisone has been used to great advantage in the treatment of disease. In allergy there is an abnormal response to an agent which would normally be non-toxic (for example inhalation of pollen, inducing asthma), and cortisone will often inhibit this change. The glucocorticoids will reduce the number of circulating eosinophils in the blood and this action has been utilized as a method of bio-assay of the hormone. Further, it has been found that cortisone will induce the lysis of lymphocytes, both those circulating and those in the lymph nodes, resulting in the release of gamma globulins which may be an important source of antibodies. To induce these changes therapeutic quantities have to be administered, about 100 mg. of cortisone a day; the normal daily output is in the region of 30 mg.

Prolonged administration of therapeutic doses of cortisone will inhibit ACTH secretion and eventually the adrenal cortex will atrophy. If therapy should suddenly be withdrawn, the patient will be left in a state of acute adrenal insufficiency and may die. In addition, if therapy is continued for some time, the patient will develop those previously described changes associated with an excess of glucocorticoids. When the hormone is used as replacement therapy in patients with absent, or diseased, adrenals, physiological quantities are given and the problems associated with therapeutic doses are not seen.

Analogues of cortisone have been synthesized which weight for weight are much more powerful than the hormone. Some have virtually no mineralocorticoid activity and are of great therapeutic value. Other analogues mainly have mineralocorticoip activity and have replaced DOC: aldosterone is not yet commercially available. Further, it has been possible to produce substances (spironolactones) of a similar chemical composition to aldosterone but which block its action at the kidney level.

(B) METATHERIA

The adrenal cortex, in histological structure, is very similar to that of the Eutherian gland, but in the opossum there is a specialized collection of cells on one side which alters during pregnancy and lactation. These cells are in many ways comparable to the X zone of the mouse adrenal.

Little is known of the function of the gland in this class. Adrenalectomy in the Rottnest Island wallaby results in anorexia, weakness, collapse, a rise of the plasma potassium with a fall of the sodium; and within some 36 hours death usually occurs. In contrast, removal of the adrenals in the American opossum is not followed by changes in the plasma sodium. It does appear that in the opossum the adrenal cortex is not as important in maintaining sodium balance as it is in the Eutherian mammal. Nevertheless, the adrenalectomized opossum does fail to retain excess salt, and after some time the blood potassium rises.

(C) PROTOTHERIA

Knowledge of the adrenal cortex in the monotremata is limited mainly to some histological observations. In the spiny anteater (Tachyglossus) the adrenal is on the medial aspect of the cranial end of the kidney, but in other classes it may be alongside. In the platypus the chromaffin tissue is abundant and, while it extends freely into the cortical cells, it has a connective tissue capsule. The cortex may be, as in mammals, divided into three zones, but in the spiny anteater the cortex is undifferentiated and resembles that of the reptiles.

BIRDS

Anatomy. In most birds the adrenals are discrete paired organs, partially covered by the gonads at the anterior ends of the kidneys. In some birds the adrenals may be fused, and there may be individual variations in the same class.

Histology. The chromaffin tissue is usually intermingled with the cortical cells. The cortex consists of cords of cells with a high content of lipid and ascorbic acid, and appears in some birds to be organized into three zones, but this demarcation is not as obvious as in mammals. Frequently the zona fasciculata is narrow and may be absent; often the zona glomerulosa is well defined.

Active principles. There is evidence that the adrenal cortex contains similar, or identical, substances to corticosterone and aldosterone.

Control. After hypophysectomy the adrenal cortex atrophies, but the peripheral zone is the least affected: administration of bovine ACTH restores the gland to normal and may lead to hypertrophy. It is therefore believed that as in mammals the activity of the gland is controlled by the adenohypophysis.

Function. On current evidence it would be reasonable to assume that this gland is essential for life. Reports of the survival of adrenalectomized birds can probably be attributed to incomplete removal of the glands, as the surgical procedure is technically difficult; even minute remnants of the adrenal cortex are sufficient to maintain life, and these remnants will increase in size because the blood concentration of ACTH is high. Both adrenal cortical extracts and DOC are effective forms of therapy in adrenalectomized birds, and, in some, saline administration will prolong life. Further studies are needed to establish the biochemical disturbances that follow adrenalectomy.

REPTILES

Anatomy. The position of the adrenals varies considerably among the different groups of reptiles. In lizards and snakes they may be a little distance from the kidneys, often in close relationship with the gonads.

Histology. Anastomosing cords of cells with a high concentration of lipid form the adrenal cortex. The chromaffin cells are on the dorsal aspect of the gland and, in addition, there are islands of these cells in the cortex.

Active principles. Little is known of the active principles of the adrenal cortex.

Control. Similar experiments to those described in the section on birds have been performed on reptiles, and it is believed that the adrenal cortex is controlled by the adenohypophysis.

Function. Adrenalectomized lizards have a diminished food intake, lose weight and become paralysed; survival may be from a few hours to a few days. In the grass snakes, after removal of the adrenals there is little change for about ten days, but at this stage they quickly deteriorate and die. There is some evidence that in alligators adrenal cortical secretions are concerned with carbohydrate metabolism.

There are only a few observations on the role of the cortical hormones on mineral balance. In snakes adrenalectomy results in a loss of sodium, but there is no change in the potassium content of the body. A great deal more work is needed in this group to determine the function of the adrenal cortex.

AMPHIBIANS

Histology. The chromaffin tissue may be scattered through the cortex or gathered together in islands. As in reptiles, there are cords of cells with a high lipid content, but these cells may merge with the renal tissue. In many amphibians there is increased activity of the gland at the spawning season and its appearance may therefore vary.

Active principles. Either cortisone or corticosterone is present. It would appear likely that all possess aldosterone.

Control. As with the other classes, hypophysectomy results in adrenal cortical atrophy and the gland is restored to normal by the administration of bovine ACTH; this therapy in normal animals results in hypertrophy of the gland which may be over-stimulated and exhausted. Removal of the pituitary gland during the period of quiescence (winter months) induces little change in the cortex, indicating that at this period activity of the gland is in abeyance, whereas in the summer the same procedure results in death in a few days. It is accepted that the adenohypophysis regulates the activity of the adrenal cortex. Of interest is the observation that large doses of oestrogen stimulate the secretion of androgens by the adrenal cortex, inducing masculinization.

Function. After adrenalectomy there is progressive weakness, congestion of blood vessels in various areas of the body, the heart rate falls and the blood viscosity rises. There are, as well, disturbances of carbohydrate, mineral and water metabolism. The blood glucose falls, the glycogen stores become depleted and the absorption of glucose is impaired. Not only is the excretion of sodium increased, but the uptake of sodium by the skin decreases and the plasma sodium falls; this is associated with a rise of plasma potassium. Adrenalectomized frogs can survive in salt water, but if this is replaced by tap water they will die. Removal of the adrenals results in the frog becoming relatively intolerant to water deprivation. Nevertheless, they retain a greater quantity of administered water than normal and this excess is not distributed evenly, but accumulates in the extracellular compartment and in the cells. The isolated muscle from an adrenalectomized frog has a reduced ability to perform work. These effects are less marked during the winter than in the summer. Adrenal cortical extracts and DOC are without effect on adrenalectomized amphibians, but it is possible that aldosterone, cortisone and cortisol would be effective therapeutic agents.

In these animals the cells which correspond to the adrenal cortex of mammals are situated around the kidney, and may be referred to as the interrenal tissue; the chromaffin cells are usually separate. As there is only fragmentary evidence on the function of this gland, it will not be considered under the standard sub-headings. In both the teleosts and the elasmobranchs current evidence indicates that the adenohypophysis exerts some control over the adrenal cortex.

In teleosts the interrenals are similar in structure and histology to those of the elasmobranchs. A characteristic feature of the cells of the interrenal of teleosts is that they do not possess the typical lipid material. Examination of the plasma has revealed the presence of cortisone-like substances. In view of the profound effects of adrenal cortical hormones on mineral and water metabolism observed in the higher vertebrates, it would be reasonable to assume that the interrenal plays an important part in osmoregulation, particularly in migrating from a marine to a freshwater environment. In some salmon the blood level of glucocorticoids rises during sexual maturation, but in the male at spawning the level falls, whereas in the female there is a further rise. In the trout which has been given an excess of salt, either cortisone or DOC increases the amount of salt retained by the kidney, but there is an increased loss of sodium through the gill mechanism resulting in a net loss of electrolytes.

The interrenal tissue in elasmobranchs may be found in three main sites, midline between the kidneys, or closely applied to the cardinal veins, or on the posterior part of the kidneys. The cells are arranged irregularly and have a high lipid content. Observations on the effects of removal of the interrenals are complicated by the fact that this class of fish are difficult to keep in captivity. The few observations made indicate that removal of this tissue results in concentration of the pigment in the melanophores, contraction of the striped muscle, lassitude and death. Although it has been previously reported that removal of the interrenals does not lead to disturbances of electrolytes, recent work suggests that the plasma potassium may rise. As elasmo-branchs are marine fishes, there is little difficulty in maintaining the sodium chloride concentration of the extracellular fluid. The unique property of the kidney in re-absorbing large amounts of urea from the tubules enables these fish to maintain the osmotic pressure of the extracellular fluid even under adverse conditions. Mammalian adrenal cortical hormones administered to fish devoid of interrenals have a beneficial action. It would seem that interrenal hormones are similar to Eutherian adrenal cortical hormones.

In cyclostomes the interrenal tissue consists of scattered cells around the cardinal veins, but nothing is known of their function and control.

2 Adrenal medulla and chromaffin tissue

In all classes of vertebrates above the fishes the adrenal gland consists of cortical cells, and cells which stain brown with chromium salts—chromaffin tissue; but only in mammals is the latter a compact mass in the centre of the adrenal gland and thus may be correctly referred to as the medulla. It must be pointed out that cells which contain 5-hydroxytroptamine also give the same colour reaction with chrome salts. In some fish the chrom-affin tissue is in the interrenal, but in the majority it is scattered over the surface of the kidneys. In mammals additional chrom-affin tissue may be found in the lower part of the abdominal aorta (para-aortic glands), or in contact with sympathetic ganglia (paraganglia). The adrenal medulla, or chromaffin tissue, develops from neural crest cells which also give rise to the sympathetic ganglia and thus the chromaffin cells may be regarded as consisting of modified ganglion cells.

MAMMALS

Histology. The cells are large and ovoid, and are arranged in clusters around the blood vessels. Histochemical techniques have revealed that the two active principles are present in separate cells.

Active principles. These are adrenaline and noradrenaline. Noradrenaline (non-methylated adrenaline) is the precursor of adrenaline, but in addition it is secreted as a separate hormone. Usually adrenaline is secreted in excess of noradrenaline, but in whales the reverse is true. Both hormones belong to the chemical family of catecholamines.

Control. The secretion of the hormones is controlled by the activity of the sympathetic nerves which supply the gland. The nervous centre controlling the sympathetic nervous system is believed to be in the hypothalamus. It has been reported that stimulation of different areas of this specialized part of the brain will induce the secretion of either adrenaline, or noradrenaline, and under different physiological conditions either one, or both, are secreted.

Function. Under basal conditions the gland secretes minute quantities of the active principles and only at times of stress (that is when preparing the animal for flight or fight) are physiological amounts secreted. A common example of excitation of the adrenal medulla is illustrated when a cat is exposed to a barking dog. The adrenal medullary hormones alter the cardio-vascular system, the tone of smooth muscle and amend the metabolism to adapt the animal for flight or fight. The actions of adrenaline are summarized in the next paragraph.

There is dilatation of the bronchi, relaxation of the intestinal tract with contraction of the sphincters. These changes allow the animal to increase the pulmonary ventilation and to inhibit all unnecessary movement of the bowel. The small blood vessels of the skin and bowel are constricted, while there is dilatation of those supplying the striped muscle; in some mammals there is dilatation of the coronary vessels. Thus the blood is directed to where it is needed. The power of each cardiac contraction is increased, ensuring more complete emptying of the heart, and thus a greater volume of blood is ejected at each beat. There is as well an increase in the heart rate. These changes in the cardio-vascular system result in a rise of blood pressure. The erector pilae muscles contract, and in the furred animals the hair rises which increases their apparent size; the pupils are dilated. The liver and muscle glycogen are converted to glucose and lactate respectively[2]; the blood glucose is raised. Adrenaline differs from glucagon in that it metabolizes muscle glycogen. It is not surprising that associated with these changes the basal metabolic rate (Chapter 5) increases. The main differences between noradrenaline and adrenaline are that the latter causes certain blood vessels to dilate and has a greater effect on metabolism.

It is possible to bio-assay minute quantities of adrenaline and noradrenaline in the blood, and thus to estimate the amount in the blood vessels to and from the gland. On stimulating the nerves to the gland the concentration of hormones in the venous blood increases. This experiment helps to establish that the tissue is an endocrine gland. Removal of the adrenal medulla does not result in any apparent alteration, except to reduce the resistance of the animal to conditions of stress. Although the adrenal medulla is an endocrine gland, it may be regarded as part of the sympathetic nervous system.

Adrenaline apparently stimulates the adenohypophysis, by way of the hypothalamus, to secrete more ACTH which in turn increases the output of adrenal cortical hormones. The latter promote gluconeogenesis and would help to replenish the depleted stores of liver glycogen—reduced by an excess of adrenaline.

In man, tumours of the adrenal medulla occasionally occur, and noradrenaline is mainly secreted, but usually it only gives rise to intermittent hypertension (high blood pressure). An excess of adrenaline in man causes sweating, tremor of the limbs and often a sensation of fear which may be of impending disaster. There is also an elevation of the basal metabolic rate.

In all subsequent classes of vertebrate there is only fragmentary knowledge of the function of the chromaffin cells and this tissue is not discussed under the standard subheadings.

BIRDS

The development, histology and control of the chromaffin tissue in this class are identical to those observed in mammals. Further, adrenaline and noradrenaline have been isolated from the adrenal glands of fowls and pigeons; histochemical techniques indicate that other birds may secrete these hormones. In the domestic fowl the predominant hormone is noradrenaline.

The small blood vessels of the fowl constrict in response to adrenaline, but it is unknown whether this hormone has a vasodilator action. With small doses of adrenaline the heart rate increases, but, as in mammals, larger amounts slow the rate reflexly because the blood pressure rises. In ducks, geese and fowls, adrenaline increases the blood glucose and the intestinal muscle is inhibited; the caecum of the fowl relaxes. In doves continued administration of adrenaline leads to adrenal cortical hypertrophy, possibly by stimulating the adenohypophysis to secrete more ACTH.

It is believed that under basal conditions only small quantities of medullary hormones are secreted, but under emergency states the output rises. Thus the effects and secretion of adrenaline are essentially similar to those in the mammalian series.

In the house sparrow (*Passer domesticus*) adrenaline suppresses the development of the gonads in both sexes. It has been suggested that this action of adrenaline plays an important physiological role in reproduction. At breeding time the increased activity of the birds results in greater quantities of adrenaline being utilized and less reaches the gonads, insufficient to maintain their suppressing action. It is probable that under normal conditions insufficient hormone is released to produce these effects and the antigonadal action of large doses is indirectly mediated by reducing the food intake.

REPTILES AND AMPHIBIANS

Chromaffin cells, as in the other classes, receive nerve fibres from the autonomic nervous system. Injections of adrenaline into frogs induce a rise of blood pressure, due to vasoconstriction, and the pigment in the melanophores is concentrated to produce pallor (Chapter 10). The action of adrenaline in both classes of vertebrate is essentially similar to that observed in mammals. This hormone is also secreted by the subcutaneous glands of the giant toad (*Bufo marinus*).

In the majority of elasmobranchs the chromaffin cells, which are separate from the interrenal tissue (the homologue of the adrenal cortex), are intimately associated with the sympathetic ganglia. The interrenal and chromaffin cells in the teleosts may be closely associated, and in *Cottus* the chromaffin cells are enclosed by the interrenal as in the higher vertebrates. The chromaffin cells have a high content of noradrenaline.

On the isolated heart adrenaline or noradrenaline increases both the rate and amplitude. Adrenaline dilates the blood vessels of the gills, but constricts the vessels of the tail and the overall effect is one of vasoconstriction. While adrenaline increases the blood glucose, it does not elevate the basal metabolic rate. As with the other endocrine glands, further work is needed to determine the role of the catecholamines in the poikilothermic vertebrates.

Summary

In the mammals and birds it is believed that the adrenal cortex is essential for life and the secretion of adrenal cortical hormones is in part controlled by the adenohypophysis. It is likely that this is true for the lower vertebrates. On the present evidence it would seem that the same adrenal cortical hormones are secreted by all the vertebrates, that is aldosterone and either cortisone (or the closely related cortisol) or corticosterone. It is not possible to differentiate between the classes of vertebrates according to whether corticosterone, or cortisone, is secreted by the adrenal cortex. Whether in all vertebrates these hormones promote the renal re-absorption of sodium and the secretion of potassium, and gluconeogenesis, has yet to be established.

In the mammalian foetus there is indirect evidence that the adrenal cortex may be functioning as an endocrine gland, probably at about the last third of the gestation period. The rat has been relatively well investigated and at about the seventeenth day of gestation (parturition occurs at the twenty-first day) the foetal adrenal cortex is capable of secretion. This is also true of the chick embryo after twelve days' incubation, and in the amphibians the embryonic adrenal may function at an even earlier stage of development.

Throughout the Vertebrata it would appear that adrenaline and noradrenaline are secreted by the chromaffin cells under the influence of the nervous system. Moreover, the actions of the hormone are essentially similar, although there are some small differences. It would appear that in fishes noradrenaline is secreted in greater quantities than adrenaline, but the reverse is true in the majority of mammals. In the mammalian foetus the main hormone is noradrenaline and usually after birth the medulla acquires the ability to methylate the noradrenaline. In man it is likely that by about the twenty-fourth week the foetus is capable of synthesizing noradrenaline.

Noradrenaline may also be regarded as a local hormone as it is secreted by the sympathetic nerve endings. This leads to a consideration of local hormones, which are dealt with in Chapter 9.

5

The thyroid gland

THE thyroid gland is a specialized tissue which selectively absorbs iodide from the blood and forms an iodinated amino acid. Of all the endocrine glands, this is the only one in which there is an extracellular store of the hormone within the gland. While the functions of the thyroid gland in mammals are reasonably well established, and in birds there is a fair knowledge, a great deal more experimental work is still necessary to determine the role and control of this gland in the cold-blooded vertebrates. Throughout the vertebrates there are some common features, namely the histology, the active principles and the special role of iodine metabolism, and these are described before the different classes are considered.

Histology. The gland is made up of cubical cells arranged in vesicles (acini) in which there is a colloid (the solid dispersed in the solvent, giving the appearance of glue) which stains red with haemotoxylin and eosin. The colloid is secreted from the surface of the epithelium into the lumen of the acinus (merocrine secretion). Holocrine secretion, that is the actual desquamation of cells into the lumen, probably does not occur in the higher vertebrates. The colloid consists of a protein (thyroglobulin) on to which thyroid hormone is bound. Between the acini there are blood vessels, lymphatics and strands of lymph tissue.

Active principles. Basically, thyroid hormone consists of iodine conjugated with tyrosine. It was believed that thyroid hormone consisted of a conjugation of two molecules of tyrosine combined with four atoms of iodine—tetra-iodothyronine or thyroxine. Recent evidence suggests that the hormone in mammals may be tri-iodothyronine, as in this class it is more potent than thyroxine and it is claimed that tri-iodothyronine acts within a few hours of administration (the effects of thyroxine are delayed for several days). Possibly thyroxine is converted by the tissues to tri-iodo-thyronine before it can exert its action. Tri-iodothyronine and thyroxine are found in the thyroid gland and blood of mammals. Whatever the composition of thyroid hormone, it is either secreted by the thyroid cells into the acinus and then bound to protein in the lumen, or the cells oxidize the iodide to iodine, and this element passes into the colloid where the hormone is synthesized; possibly the colloid itself is capable of reducing iodide to iodine. The hormone is liberated from this store by hydrolysis, and secreted into the blood stream, where the major portion is bound to the plasma protein. In the rat the affinity of protein binding with thyroxine is four times greater than that with tri-iodothyronine, which is approximately the inverse of their relative activities. In man the hormone is bound mainly to globulin and to a small degree to albumin, but in some other mammals the main binding is with albumin.

There is some evidence that thyroxine can be formed by the tissues of the body, and it has been observed that if a high concentration of iodine (well above physiological levels) is incubated with plasma protein or casein, thyroxine is synthesized.

In the submammalian classes, only thyroxine has been identified in the thyroid gland. In the poikilothermic vertebrates the rate of synthesis of the hormone is relatively slow.

Iodine. This element is essential for the formation of thyroid hormone. The thyroid gland possesses the specialized ability to take up relatively large amounts of iodide from the blood, and in the cells, or in the colloid, this is oxidized to iodine which is used in the synthesis of the hormone. Therefore it is not surprising to find that as much as 0.06% by weight of this trace element is found in this gland of mammals. It is possible to depress the cellular mechanism of accumulating iodide with relatively non-toxic agents, such as thiocyanate and perchlorate. This treatment results in decreased synthesis of thyroid hormone. Further, the affinity of the thyroid gland for iodine may be used as a test of its activity. By using radioactive iodine and a suitable detector over the gland the relative rate of accumulation of the element can be determined. Under standard conditions and in general terms a high or low uptake, respectively, indicates excessive or depressed activity of the gland.

The thyroid gland develops from the floor of the embryonic mouth as a midline diverticulum which grows downwards. The bifurcated end gives rise to the centre and part of the lateral lobes, while the remainder is derived from the fourth pharyngeal pouch. The duct connecting the thyroid to the mouth is called the thyroglossal duct and it usually disappears early in development. Accessory thyroid tissue may be found anywhere along the line of the original thyroglossal duct.

Control. As already discussed (Chapter 2), there is a reciprocal relationship between TSH and thyroid hormone. Not only does TSH control the rate of formation and secretion of the hormone, but it also acts as a stimulus to the growth of the thyroid cells and thus is comparable with the actions of ACTH on the adrenal cortex. An excess of TSH induces the cubical epithelium to become columnar and branch into the colloid; the amount of the colloid diminishes. If there is a deficiency of TSH the cubical cells become flattened and the amount of colloid increases. Individual acini may fuse with one another to produce large colloidal masses.

Function. It would appear likely that even in the embryo the thyroid functions as an endocrine gland and the time at which this occurs varies from one-third to nine-tenths of the gestation period. The main action of thyroid hormone is to control the metabolic rate of the body under resting conditions (basal metabolic rate) and, as heat is produced in metabolism, it is one of the mechanisms maintaining body temperature.

The basal metabolic rate may be simply defined as the energy required by the animal at mental and physical rest, and is a measure of the activity of the thyroid. Energy is liberated in the cells by metabolizing materials in the presence of oxygen, and it is possible to relate the volume of oxygen consumed to calories released. Hence the rate of utilization of oxygen can be used to measure the basal metabolic rate. It has been suggested that the primary action of the thyroid hormone is to control the rate of oxidation in the cells.

A fall of the basal metabolic rate, as occurs in thyroid deficiency, would result in a fall of the heart rate, and the respiration may be slowed; in man, in this climate, the body temperature may fall. As less of the ingested food is metabolized, there is more available for conversion to body fat and the animal gains weight. The diminished metabolism of the cells of the cerebral cortex results in a prolonged reaction time. This slowed cerebration is readily recognized in man by the delay taken in answering simple questions and, unless care is taken to allow sufficient time to answer, it may be incorrectly assumed that there is a mental defect. It is of interest to add that thyroid deficiency may lead to a true mental disturbance.

If there is an insufficiency of thyroid hormone in man, there is an accumulation of a mucoid substance in the tissues which is referred to as myxoedematous tissue. This tissue may occur beneath the skin of the whole body, but it is usually most marked in the face and hands. These changes may occur in the larynx giving rise to the characteristic husky voice of the hypothyroid patient; less frequently the middle ear may be involved, resulting in deafness. In view of this particular change in the subcutaneous tissues in thyroid deficiency, the hypothyroid state in man is called myxoedema. Myxoedematous tissue on histological examination superficially resembles Wharton's jelly in the umbilicus of the foetus, but this change cannot be regarded as a maturation defect. In myxoedema there may be a deficiency of the number of circulating red cells and it has been claimed that this is due to a maturation defect in their development.

Thyroid hormone is responsible for the normal growth of the young animal. In the absence of the hormone there is mental, physical and sexual retardation; in general terms this may be regarded as a maturation defect. The influence of the thyroid hormone on the central nervous system is widespread. As discussed earlier, hypothyroidism may impair cerebration, and it is likely that in several classes the hormone is essential for normal development of the brain (for example in the rat). The reflex contraction of striped muscle following stretch is characteristically delayed in thyroid deficiency, and this is in part due to some impairment of neuromuscular transmission.

Probably, in controlling body growth it acts either in conjunction with, or sensitizes the tissues to, STH. In many mammalian classes the growth and eruption of the teeth are determined by the activity of the thyroid, and in the deer it enhances the growth of the antlers. In the rat and guinea-pig it has been shown that thyroid hormone controls the growth of hair; in man absence of the hormone results in baldness which has a typical distribution. In the female, thyroid deficiency reduces fertility, prolongs the period of anoestrus, reduces the milk yield and may cause abortion. Fertility is also reduced in the male, as there is impaired spermatogenesis.

Thyroid deficiency is a relatively uncommon disease in man. It may occur because the cells of the gland fail to respond to TSH, or because the adenohypophysis does not secrete the trophic hormone, or because the iodide intake is insufficient. If there is insufficient iodide in the diet, the output of thyroid hormone falls and the level of TSH rises, stimulating the gland. There is cellular proliferation and enhanced activity, and a greater quantity of iodide is removed from the blood, despite the low concentration. Even with maximal stimulation of the gland it may not be possible to synthetize enough hormone to maintain the normal basal metabolic rate. The appearance of the gland may now alter from that of stimulation to exhaustion. The gland does not respond uniformly to TSH, but rather in groups of acini so that one area may be hypertrophic, while another is atrophic. Thyroid deficiency may also be due to some congenital defect of the gland, not infrequently occurring in the newborn infants of mothers with impaired thyroid function. These infants, as expected, fail to grow mentally, physically and sexually, resulting in a characteristic clinical appearance to which the name cretin is given. Cretins are short, pot-bellied and fat; the tongue protrudes out of the mouth, from which excess saliva flows. They are mentally impaired, but are of pleasant disposition. Provided thyroid hormone is administered in the early months of infancy, this defect may be rectified, but if given during early childhood, when the appearance is characteristic, only physical and sexual growth may occur. In the adult myxoedema is easily recognizable. The patients are fat and the hair on the head is scanty. The skin of the face has a 'dry parchment' appearance. The myxoedematous changes under the skin render the face relatively immobile. The nose and lips are thickened: the eyelids are puffy and the eyebrows are thin. These changes result in a typical appearance. The patients are slow both in movement and thought, often huddled in blankets, complaining in their husky voices of the cold on a summer day.

There are miscellaneous actions of thyroid hormone which are considered in this paragraph. An action of thyroid hormone which is ill understood is that controlling body water. In thyroid deficiency there is an increase in interstitial body water and a fall in the daily urine volume, whereas with thyroid excess there is a polyuria (excessive excretion of urine). The role of the thyroid in hibernating mammals remains uncertain, but, while it does not play a dominant part, thyroid inactivity does contribute to the induction of this state. As thyroid hormone promotes growth, it must to some extent increase protein anabolism, but in excess it causes catabolism. In man thyroid excess leads to increased quantities of creatinine being excreted, and significant quantities of creatine appear in the urine; both substances are of importance in the energy requirements for muscular contraction. This may account for the muscular weakness observed in hyperthyroidism (an excess of thyroid hormone). By some unknown action thyroid hormone significantly alters the level of the blood cholesterol, lack or excess raising or lowering the level respectively. The hormone to some small degree increases gluconeogenesis and promotes glucose absorption from the bowel; thus thyroid deficiency decreases the blood glucose, while an excess raises it. Compensating mechanisms will tend, however, to obscure this effect.

The activity of the thyroid increases in man during puberty and adolescence, and there may be an enlargement of the thyroid gland at this period. The gland is also stimulated or depressed by a cold or hot environment respectively. This is of great importance in adaptation. An increase of the basal metabolic rate will result in a greater production of heat energy, which will be of value in a cold climate, and the reverse applies in a hot climate. Any increase in the visible size of the thyroid gland is called goitre and it may occur with physiological changes, iodine deficiency, myxoedema or with hyperthyroidism.

Hyperthyroidism occurs relatively frequently in man, and is more common in the female. The condition is caused either by over-production of TSH, the hypothalamus or adenohypophysis failing to respond to the inhibiting action of thyroid hormone, or to the thyroid gland becoming autonomous and secreting an excess of its hormone. In both conditions there is an elevation of the basal metabolic rate and this results in a loss of weight, as usually the food intake is insufficient to meet the needs of the enhanced metabolism. (The terms primary and secondary hyper-thyroidism used in clinical medicine are of no real value.) In temperate climates the temperature does not rise, as compensating mechanisms operate to dissipate the excess heat produced, for example the blood vessels of the skin dilate and there is increased sweating. If the environmental temperature rises, heat loss from the body may be impossible and the body temperature will rise. As expected, the pulse rate increases, but there is little change in the respiratory rate. The normal reaction time is not shortened, as an increase in metabolism cannot shorten this time. An excess of thyroid hormone sensitizes the tissues to adrenaline. Under these circumstances the normal small quantities of circulating adrenaline are sufficient to produce the effects of over-dosage, that is, sweating, tremor, increased heart rate and the sensation of impending disaster. The enhanced excitability, irritability and emotional lability observed with excess thyroid hormone may be due to this action. The clinical picture is that of a thin, tremulous, emotional person with a flushed sweaty skin, who appears startled owing to retraction of the upper eyelids. In certain patients with thyrotoxicosis (hyperthyroidism) there is as well a forward protrusion of the eyeballs (exophthalmos), induced it is believed by an excess of TSH acting on the retro-orbital tissues to increase the fat and fluid content. Patients often complain of fatigue, and muscular weakness may be very severe.

Methods of assessing thyroid function. A convenient indirect

D

method is to measure the basal metabolic rate, as this is simply performed by estimating the oxygen consumption in unit time, during physical and mental rest. The known avidity of the thyroid gland for iodine forms the basis of another test—the rate of accumulation of radioactive iodine: conditions other than thyrotoxicosis, namely deficiency of iodine, can result in an increased uptake of this element. As the iodine bound to the plasma protein is mainly in the form of thyroid hormone, the amount of iodine in the precipitated plasma proteins is a reliable index of the quantity of circulating hormone.

BIRDS

The development of the gland is essentially similar to that of the mammals.

Control. This aspect has not been as carefully investigated as in mammals, but it is believed that the thyroid gland is under the control of the adenohypophysis; further, the same inverse relationship exists between the levels of thyroid hormone and TSH.

Function. During spring and summer there is histological evidence of diminished activity, while in winter and autumn activity is enhanced, and it is believed that a fall of environmental temperature stimulates the gland. In this class there are specialized functions of the thyroid hormone. First, it is believed to exercise some control over pre-migration activity, as administration of the hormone will induce this state. Secondly, the moult is influenced by the level of thyroid hormone. An excess precipitates the onset of moulting, while thyroidectomy prevents its normal occurrence, but there is a marked variation among different species, the crows and jackdaws being relatively resistant; the sensitivity may vary in the same bird in different parts of the body. Thirdly, the hormone controls the growth of new feathers. Thyroidectomy in domestic hens leads to a feathering with very few barbules and the cock-feather pattern is produced; oestrogen administration will not restore the hen type of feathers. On the colour of feathers the effect varies in different classes, but in the Brown Leghorn cock thyroidectomy leads to the replacement of the black pigment (melanin) by a red-brown one. Fourthly, broodiness is in part due to increased thyroid activity. Lastly, it would appear that thyroxine is to some degree responsible for the growth of the spurs and the comb of cockerels.

It is believed that in this class, as in mammals, the basal metabolic rate, maturation and growth are controlled by thyroid hormone. Following the administration of thyroxine to birds there is a rise of the blood glucose, red cell count and an increase of the heart rate; the latter may be due to an increased sensitivity to adrenaline.

Thyroidectomy leads to failure of gonadal development in the young, and even in the adult there is atrophy, but in starlings it is claimed that this procedure stimulates the gonads. Thyroxine stimulates testicular development in male ducks, and in domestic fowls; there is good evidence that the hormone stimulates egg production in hens. In general it would appear that thyroid hormone is essential for the normal function of the gonads. In excess, the hormone may not only inhibit TSH, but also gonadotrophic secretion, resulting in atrophy of the gonads.

REPTILES AND AMPHIBIANS

The gland develops from the upper part of the pharynx.

Control. It is believed that in these classes of vertebrates, the activity of the thyroid is controlled by the adenohypophysis, but it is not known whether the blood concentration of TSH and thyroid hormone are inversely related to one another, as in mammals.

Function. In amphibians the classical view is that metamorphosis of the tadpole is under the control of the thyroid gland and a critical level of the hormone is necessary for normal maturation. A remarkable claim is that failure to metamorphose in the Israeli spadefoot (*Pelobates syriacus*) is due to the absence of the thyroid gland. In some other amphibians development is normally arrested at the larval stage. In the axolotl, where thyroid administration will lead to metamorphosis, there is a relative insensitivity of the tissues to thyroxine. In some salamanders failure to metamorphose appears to be due to lack of tissue responsiveness to the hormone.[3]

In salamanders and newts thyroxine administration inhibits experimental limb regeneration and, even if it is given after the commencement of growth, after an initial stimulus there is no further growth. There is no clear evidence that thyroid hormone controls the growth of epiphyseal bones in these classes of vertebrates. In tadpoles thyroidectomy increases growth, while administered thyroxine will inhibit it.

There is little information on the role of thyroid hormone in reptiles, but it is likely that aggressiveness, particularly at the breeding season, may be controlled by this hormone. In both reptiles and amphibians thyroid hormone does not significantly affect the metabolic rate, but it appears to be essential for normal nervous activity.

Administration of thyroxine leads to desquamation of the cornified cells of the epidermis, with resultant thinning of the skin; this, together with increased vascularity, enhances the value of the skin as a respiratory organ.

FISHES

Thyroid tissue may not only be found in the upper part of the pharynx, but also anywhere along the ventral aorta, and in various other sites. In teleosts thyroid tissue may be present in the eyes, brain, kidney and spleen. In some elasmobranchs and teleosts the thyroid may be encapsulated.

Histology. This is basically similar to that of other vertebrates but in some elasmobranchs the epithelium may be ciliated. Disintegrating epithelial cells may be seen in the colloid.

Control. As far as it is known, this is the same as in the other poikilothermic vertebrates.

Function. As with other cold-blooded vertebrates, the thyroid has no effect on metabolic rate, although it is claimed that thyroxine administration to the goldfish increases the oxygen consumption. Failure to demonstrate a metabolic effect with this hormone may be due to technical difficulties, for example handling, but nevertheless it is relatively easy to demonstrate an increase of oxygen consumption with testosterone or dinitrophenol.

Thyroid hormone apparently stimulates differential growth, possibly by acting in conjunction with STH, during development so that the proportions of the fins, body weight and length are altered, but there is little doubt that in some species the hormone does not influence growth. Administration of thyroxine may result in abnormal growth of the head, due to overgrowth of osteogenic (bony) and retro-orbital tissues. The hormone may control mineral metabolism by decreasing saline tolerance, but the role of the thyroid in osmoregulation is still uncertain and this uncertainty also applies to the control of migration.

Thyroxine can influence skin changes. If it is given to salmon and trout the deposition of guanine is increased and they become 'silvery'; sometimes 'silvering' is induced in fish that normally do not show this change. In sturgeons the hormone accelerates scale formation. In small doses thyroxine promotes protein anabolism, but with larger doses there is catabolism.

There may be seasonal activity of the thyroid gland, which in the salmon can be related to the number of hours of daylight, peak activity occurring in the summer. In the trout, as in mammals, thyroid activity increases with a fall in the temperature, unlike many of the fish in which there is a positive correlation between activity of the gland and temperature; in some it would appear that temperature change induces no alteration.

Some fishes, namely mud-skippers (*Periophthalmus*), assume a semi-terrestrial life the onset of which appears to be accelerated by administering thyroxine.[31] It would appear that transition in the mode of activity and structure observed in some fish, and often referred to as metamorphosis, is not under the direct control of the thyroid gland. In the lamprey attempts to induce 'metamorphosis' with thyroxine have been unsuccessful and the change from the larval to adult form is independent of thyroid hormone.

The larval lamprey is of interest as here the thyroid gland is the endostyle which secretes not only the hormone, but also mucus. The hormone flows into the pharynx and thence into the alimentary canal where intestinal proteolytic enzymes free the thyroxine from the protein. In the adult lamprey the duct into the pharynx closes, but now the gland apparently possesses proteo-lytic enzymes which are capable of freeing the hormone from the protein, as in the other classes.

Summary

The well-known property of thyroid hormone in controlling the basal metabolic rate is only observed in the homoiothermic vertebrates, and in this class the hormone is also responsible for mental, sexual and physical growth. In the poikilothermic verte-brates the hormone does appear to be of importance in differenti-ation, particularly of the central nervous system, and in some classes it may influence growth. Unexpectedly, it is not the metabolic action but that influencing neuronal activity which is the common action of the thyroid hormone throughout the vertebrate series. This hormone probably exercises some control over both nerve conduction and excitability, and general behaviour.[3]

The thyroid gland is only one of several structures, namely the salivary and gastric glands and chloride cells of the gills, that develop from the upper part of the alimentary canal and which are able to transport iodides, or halides: the breast and the kidney also possess this property.

It is tempting to speculate that the thyroid gland developed from a primitive salivary gland which acquired the specialized function of allowing a sufficiently high concentration of iodine to accumulate, and thus allowed thyroid hormone synthesis to be reasonably efficient. It has been suggested that thyroid hormone, as it occurs in some of the present-day invertebrates (annelids and molluscs), was available in the evolutionary scale before the development of the gland and possibly before there was tissue responsiveness to this hormone. The development of the thyroid gland, by providing a store of this hormone, has enabled the animal to adapt successfully during periods of low iodine intake.

6

The parathyroid glands

IN BIRDS, reptiles and amphibians the parathyroids develop from the ventral corners of the second, third and fourth pharyngeal pouches. In mammals they are derived from the dorsal corners of the third and fourth. This difference in development has apparently no functional significance. In fishes the parathyroids are absent and this provides the exception to the general finding that comparable endocrine glands are present throughout the vertebrate series. The ultimobranchial body of the fish develops from that embryonic tissue which in tetrapods gives rise to the parathyroids. Further, there are isolated observations which would suggest that this body may secrete parathormone, but at present there is no definite evidence to support this claim.

MAMMALS

Usually the parathyroids consist of four oval bodies situated in the neck in close proximity to the back of the thyroid—one at each pole. The rat, mouse, shrew, hedgehog and pig only have two parathyroids. In man there are usually four parathyroids, but their position and number may vary and this tissue may be found lower in the neck or even in the thorax.

Histology. The glands are about 6 mm in length in man, oval in shape, and they may be embedded in the thyroid tissue, but are well encapsulated. The vascular supply is profuse, but the nerve supply scanty. The gland is made up of closely packed epithelial cells, which in man and some mammals consist of two types: (a) principal, or chief, cells that are cuboidal, contain nongranular cytoplasm with faintly staining nuclei, and secrete the hormone; (b) eosinophil cells which are larger, contain eosino-philic granules in the cytoplasm and have well-demarcated nuclei. The latter cells only appear just prior to, or at, puberty in man, but their function is unknown.

Active principles. In 1925 Collip[22] prepared an active extract of high molecular weight (650,000) which behaved like a protein: this substance was named parathormone. Recently it has been shown that the activity is contained in a much smaller molecule; a polypeptide of molecular weight at least 8,600 is probably the hormone.[53] Another principle, calcitonin, has been isolated.

Control. It would appear that the rate of secretion of parathor-mone is controlled by the level of the blood calcium: a fall of blood calcium stimulating and a rise suppressing the activity of the gland. Investigations carried out in the last few years indicate that the adenohypophysis may exert some control over the secretion of parathormone.

Function. Parathormone controls the level of the blood cal-cium and there are two main ways in which this is achieved. First, it prevents phosphate re-absorption by the kidney tubules, increasing the amount excreted, and the blood level of this ion falls. There is a reciprocal relationship between the levels of calcium and phosphate in the blood (a fall of the phosphate level leading to an increase in the calcium level). Thus by this mechan-ism parathormone indirectly controls the blood calcium level.[9] Secondly, parathormone causes mobilization of calcium and phosphate from bones, and the blood calcium rises.[50] It would seem that the hormone controls the dynamic equilibrium which exists between the extracellular fluid and the bone. It was origin-ally believed that the first action of parathormone was the im-portant one, as the sequence of events following the administra-tion of parathormone is—increased phosphate excretion, a fall of blood phosphate level, a rise of blood calcium level and lastly an increased excretion of calcium (the high blood level of this ion results in an increased amount being filtered and excreted by the kidney). Nevertheless, there is little doubt that the hormone has a direct action on bone and the two actions of the hormone cannot be separated. If considered alone, the action of the hormone on bone would elevate both the blood phosphate and calcium levels, but by the kidney action excess phosphate is excreted, and the observed changes are an elevation of the calcium with a fall of the phosphate level. It has been suggested that the hormone may have a third action, promoting the absorption of calcium from the alimentary canal, and it would in this respect resemble the action of vitamin D.[30]

Removal of the parathyroids results in a fall in the blood calcium level; and in man tetany occurs within a few days. In both man and carnivorous animals this gland is essential for life. Hypoparathyroidism is rare in clinical medicine, but the common cause is the occasional accidental removal of these glands during thyroidectomy. Tetany in man usually consists of spasms of the muscles of the hands, feet and larynx, the muscle spasm in the hands producing the characteristic position (*main d'accoucheur*); in addition there may be generalized convulsions. The muscle spasms are believed to be due to increased excitability of the motor nerve fibres, induced by the low level of the blood calcium, and they occur when this falls below 7 mg/100 ml (normal level 9–11). If the blood calcium level is below normal, it is possible to demonstrate the enhanced excitability of the motor nerves by compressing the upper arm to occlude the arterial flow for a short period, when the muscles of the hand will go into their characteristic spasm (Trousseau's sign); or by tapping the facial nerve and observing that the muscles of the face contract for a brief period (Chvostek's sign). If one or both of these signs are present, without spontaneous tetany, the condition is called latent tetany. A fall of the blood calcium is accompanied by a decrease in the blood magnesium level and it has been suggested that the low level of the latter element makes a significant contribution to the increased excitability of the motor nerves.

The opposite condition to hypoparathyroidism may occur spontaneously in man induced by a tumour of the gland secreting an excess of parathormone. This results in not only general demineralization of the bones, but also the protein matrix may be absorbed, resulting in bone cysts, and the blood calcium rises. Ectopic calcification occurs in the kidneys, arteries, stomach and lungs: in addition there are gastro-intestinal disturbances and generalized weakness.

In cattle, tetany does not occur after removal of the parathyroids and cattle are resistant to the administration of parathormone. This hormone is apparently of little importance in
these animals.

As parathormone is concerned with the blood level of calcium,
it is necessary to consider this ion in greater detail. In the blood,
calcium exists in two forms, approximately one-half dialysable,
the crystalloid (not bound to protein), and one-half non-
dialysable (bound to protein). The major portion of the crystalloid is ionized, and it is only the ionized form of calcium which
is of physiological importance. The ionized and non-ionized calcium are in a state of dynamic equilibrium and this equilibrium
is to a large extent controlled by the hydrogen ion concentration.
A rise in pH (decrease of H ions) results in a decrease in the
quantity of ionized calcium. Hence alkalosis (an increase in the
amount of alkali in the blood) will induce tetany, as the amount
of ionized calcium is reduced, although the total may be normal.
As well, alkalosis acts directly to increase nerve excitability. A
simple way to induce alkalosis is to over-breathe and remove the
acid-forming carbon dioxide from the blood.

Until recently parathormone was only available in a relatively
impure form as a protein. Repeated administration of parathormone resulted in antibodies being produced in the recipient
which inactivated the hormone. This fact has made investigations into the long-term effects of the hormone impossible and
has markedly restricted the use of parathormone in the treatment
of tetany.

Calcitonin, it is claimed, lowers the blood calcium and opposes
the action of parathormone. There is some evidence in favour
of the existence of this principle in the dog. Extensive investiga-
ions are needed to establish whether calcitonin is a hormone and
whether it is derived from the thyroid or parathyroid glands.

BIRDS

There are two glands on either side of the neck in the pigeon,
duck and fowl (the only birds which have been extensively
studied). In the fowl the two parathyroids on one side may fuse

and there may be accessory parathyroid tissue in the thymus. In other groups of birds there is only one parathyroid on each side of the neck.

Histology. The gland consists of epithelial cells, which correspond to the principal cells of mammals, arranged in cords, but there are no eosinophil, or oxyphil, cells.

Active principle. It is assumed that this is basically identical with mammalian parathormone.

Control. This is probably the same as in mammals, and in ducks it has been shown that hypophysectomy results in a reduction in the size of the gland.

Function. Parathormone acts in an essentially similar fashion to that observed in mammals, controlling metabolism of calcium in the bones and blocking the re-absorption of phosphate by the kidney tubules; but only three kinds of bird have been investigated in any detail. Certainly in the duck and pigeon removal of the parathyroids results in convulsions, and in about twenty-four hours the birds die; the fall in blood calcium can be prevented by the administration of parathormone. In the fowl the effects of parathyroidectomy are in dispute, as some observers report that convulsions occur, while others have failed to obtain this effect. This discrepancy can probably be explained by the fact that in this bird there may be accessory parathyroid tissue.

In the normal pigeon administration of parathormone results in an elevation of the blood calcium level, but little change is induced in the duck. There is a great deal of disagreement on the effects of parathormone in birds, probably because the hormone is of mammalian origin; the hormone derived from birds might give more consistent results.

In the female duck oestrogen administration leads to an elevation of the blood calcium, but it is without effect in the parathyroidectomized animal. In the pigeon oestrogen has this action on calcium metabolism in the absence of parathormone. Thus the role of the parathyroids in the elevation of the blood calcium and deposition of calcium in medullary bones, seen in female birds prior to egg laying, is still uncertain. It is of interest that in the fowl, duck and pigeon any method which reduces the amount of calcium entering the body leads to hypertrophy of the parathyroids, as in carnivorous mammals.

REPTILES AND AMPHIBIANS

The gland in these classes is less vascular and the cellular component is more compact than that of the homoiothermic vertebrates. In amphibians during the cold season the parathyroids show histological evidence of inactivity and even degenerative changes; in the bullfrog these changes may be very marked.

In amphibians the effects of parathyroidectomy vary. This procedure in bullfrogs (*Rana catesbiana*) results in a fall of blood calcium, increased neuromuscular irritability and death —changes comparable with those seen in carnivorous mammals. Some frogs and salamanders show no ill effects after parathyroidectomy. There is a fall in the level of blood calcium in a frog (*Rana pipiens*), but no evidence of increased neuromuscular irritability.

It is to be hoped that further work will be carried out on the poikilothermic vertebrates, particularly the reptiles where little information is available.

Summary

Only in man has there been an extensive study of the physiology of the parathyroids, and in other mammals there are large gaps in our knowledge. In birds and the poikilothermic tetrapods only isolated facts are known. The resistance of cattle to the procedure of parathyroidectomy may be due to the presence of accessory parathyroids, but this is obviously difficult to establish. In man and the carnivorous mammals parathormone is necessary to maintain the blood calcium level, and this in turn is essential for normal nervous excitability—indeed it may influence the excitability and activity of all tissues. In these classes the absence of parathormone results in death in a few days.

7

The islets of Langerhans

THE hormones from the pancreas enter the portal blood stream and are carried to the liver. Enzymes exist in the liver which inactivate these hormones and thus a small but unknown quantity enters the systemic circulation. It would appear that the main action of these hormones is on the liver cells. Further, any attempt to compare the actions of these hormones, when large quantities are administered into the peripheral circulation, with the hormones that are normally secreted by the islet cells is not likely to be valid. The hormones exert some control over glucose metabolism which is a fundamental process of the living cell.

The development of the pancreas is basically similar in all the vertebrates. From the intestinal wall there is one dorsal root and two ventral roots which unite; later the dorsal root usually disappears. The roots grow into the mesentery and from the budding tubules cells develop, which if they retain their connection with the tubules become acini, while those that are isolated develop into islets. In the ammocoete larva (for example the lamprey) the primitive roots do not grow into the mesentery and the islets remain in the wall of the alimentary canal. It is possible that in the higher vertebrates thate mey be islet tissue in the small intestine.

In all classes below mammals, little is known about the control of the secretion of the active principles; it is likely that these are essentially the same in all vertebrates, but the relative importance of each active principle may vary within and between the different classes. Thus, the standard subheadings of active principles and control are not followed when considering the submammalian classes.

MAMMALS

A disease in man known as diabetes mellitus (a running through or siphoning of honey water) has been recognized for thousands of years, and it is the commonest endocrine abnormality. It was not until 1889 that von Mering and Minkowski[46] were able to produce a similar condition in dogs by removal of the pancreas. Histological examination of this structure revealed that scattered amongst the acini were islands of specialized cells (first described by Langerhans in his thesis in 1869) and in 1909 it was suggested that these cells secreted a hormone, the absence of which induced the diabetic state. As the cells are in islands, the hormone was named insuline.[25] The hormone was not isolated until 1922 and was then, as now, referred to as insulin.[13]

Anatomy. In man the head of the pancreas is on the right, in close proximity to the inner curve of the duodenum; the body is in contact with lumbar vertebrae while the tail stretches to the left. The organ may be compact, as in man, or diffuse, as in the rat.

Histology. The islets are scattered throughout the pancreas, but are most numerous in the tail. Special staining techniques have shown that the islets consist mainly of two types of cells, α and β. Any single islet will contain both cells, but the β cells are by far the more numerous.

As alloxan (a derivative of uric acid) selectively destroys the β cells with the production of typical diabetic symptoms, it is accepted that insulin is secreted by these cells.

Active principles. The main hormone secreted is insulin (a complex polypeptide with molecular weight of approximately 6,000)[55] which lowers the concentration of glucose in the blood. The difficulty of isolating the hormone was that, being a complex polypeptide, it was digested and destroyed by the proteolytic enzymes of the pancreatic acini as soon as any attempt was made to extract it. This difficulty was initially overcome by tying the pancreatic duct, which resulted in the destruction of the acini in a few weeks, but this procedure left the islets unaffected, and the hormone could then be extracted.

A substance called glucagon is probably secreted by the α cells and raises the blood glucose level, but there is still a little doubt whether it is a true hormone in mammals.

Control. It is suggested that the rate of secretion of insulin is controlled by the blood glucose level, a rise stimulating and a fall depressing the rate. The adenohypophysis exerts little or no control, although, as discussed in Chapter 2, STH stimulates and ultimately destroys the islet tissue in some fully grown mammals. Evidence that the level of the blood glucose does regulate secretion is given by the following experiment. If a dog is pancreatectomized and the circulation connected to one, two or three pancreases from normal dogs, the blood glucose is normal in the pancreatectomized animal, irrespective of the number of the pancreases utilized.[3, 36]

Function. While insulin appears to have many actions, this may in part be the result of the main function of the hormone, which is to facilitate the entry of glucose at a physiological concentration into the cells. An extracellular fluid concentration of approximately 80 mg/100 ml, in the presence of insulin, is sufficient to allow glucose to enter most cells, but in the absence of the hormone the level may rise to 1000 mg/100 ml or more—that is, until a level is reached when glucose can enter the cells. The cells of the central nervous system are exceptional, as insulin is not necessary for the entry of glucose. Once the glucose is intracellular it is likely that metabolism is stimulated and glucose is rapidly converted into glycogen, or broken down to lactic acid. Insulin inhibits gluconeogenesis and thus opposes the action of adrenal cortical, adenohypophysial and thyroid hormones. It is therefore apparent that removal of the adrenal cortex or the hypophysis will reduce the severity of the diabetic condition, but the animal becomes very sensitive to insulin. Another action of insulin is to promote fat anabolism. In contrast, the action of glucagon appears to be relatively simple. It acts on the glycogen in the liver cell, breaking this down to glucose which enters the blood stream, but muscle glycogen is unaffected (cf. adrenaline).

In the absence of insulin, the blood glucose rises (hypergly-caemia) and exceeds the renal tubular capacity for re-absorption; glucose appears in the urine (glycosuria) and, as it is an osmoti-cally active substance, extra water will be excreted. The daily volume of urine excreted rises, leading to dehydration and thirst. As gluconeogenesis is uninhibited, it proceeds at an accelerated rate and body proteins, in addition to fats, are catabolized, leading to loss of weight, despite a normal or even enhanced appetite. Liver and muscle glycogen may be reduced, but the amount in the kidney tubules and heart increases. In the diabetic patient it has been found that wounds are easily infected; this may be related to the high blood glucose, as sugar is a nutrient medium for bacteria.

In order to catabolize fat normally, oxaloacetic acid is neces-sary, which is chiefly derived from glucose. The liver cells will in the absence of oxaloacetic acid condense pairs of two carbon radicals which are derived from fat to form excess quantities of acetoacetic acid, and derivatives of this, β hydroxybutyric acid and acetone; these three are referred to as ketone bodies. Thus there is a surfeit of ketone bodies in the blood and urine of patients with diabetes mellitus. If there is an excess of ketone bodies in the blood or urine, the terms used are ketonaemia or ketonuria respectively. If the ketonaemia is sufficiently intense, there is acidosis (excess acidity of the blood) despite the fact that there are mechanisms to excrete and to buffer the acid metabo-lites; also these metabolites can to a small degree be utilized by the tissues. In man with severe acidosis there is disturbed cerebra-tion, coma, and death may ensue.

The effect of removal or destruction of the islet tissue varies in different animals. In dogs death usually occurs in two to three weeks, but the pig, rabbit and calf may survive for a long time without insulin. The last three animals lose weight and glycosuria is present. Ketonaemia does not occur in rabbits and it is slight in calves; in pigs ketonaemia may be severe, yet coma does not occur. As there is some ability to utilise carbohydrates in the absence of insulin, it may be that this hormone in these three animals mainly acts to promote the storage of glucose as glycogen. In the sheep it is possible to induce severe ketonaemia, but there is considerable individual variation. It is technically difficult to remove the whole of the pancreas in the rat, but removal of some 99% (that is, virtually a total pancreatectomy) results in severe ketonaemia, glycosuria and death in one or two days. After sub-total pancreatectomy not all the rats become diabetic, and there are fewer females than males affected, but the incidence of diabetes is increased if the females are spayed. There is as yet no agreement about the effects of pancreatectomy in the rhesus monkey. Some workers find that the ketonaemia is transitory: fasting lowers the blood glucose and glycosuria disappears. Other investigators have found that this procedure results in permanent ketonaemia, high blood glucose and glycosuria, and if the latter observations are correct the effects of pancreatectomy are similar to those seen in the baboon. Insulin restores the diabetic animal to normal, but in the dog even with this therapy there is fatty infiltration of the liver, which is prevented by the administration of choline; this is the only mammal in which this change has been clearly described.[35]

In man the diabetes induced by pancreatectomy is relatively mild, but spontaneous diabetes mellitus may be a serious illness with severe ketonaemia and coma. The possible explanation for this discrepancy is that there are other factors operating besides insulin lack. A somewhat similar condition can be induced in the experimental animal, where it is found that the severity of the diabetic condition is greater in the alloxan-treated than in the pancreatectomized animal. It is likely that in the former animal, in addition to the lack of insulin, there is glucagon secretion which would elevate the blood glucose and this may account for the difference observed; but this mechanism is not the complete answer to the problem in man.

An excess of insulin lowers the blood glucose (hypoglycaemia) resulting in disturbed cerebration, coma and even death. The hypoglycaemic action of insulin is usually observed within an hour or so of administration. Occasionally in man a tumour of the islet cell occurs and there is excessive secretion of insulin. This rare condition is of interest because the mental disturbance induced by the low blood glucose may lead to these people being wrongly diagnosed as suffering from mental disease.

In most mammals that hibernate the blood glucose is low during this state. Injections of insulin into these animals will induce a condition like hibernation and they cannot easily be roused. While it is accepted that hypoglycaemia if sufficiently severe will induce unconsciousness, it would seem likely that hypoglycaemic coma and hibernation are two different conditions. The low blood glucose in hibernation merely indicates a depression of the metabolic activities.

As previously mentioned, in vertebrates below mammals the active principles secreted and the control of secretion are believed to be basically similar to those of mammals and are not considered in the subsequent sections.

BIRDS

Histology. This is similar to the mammals, but a characteristic feature is that the islets may only consist of one type of cell—either α or β. In this class there are more α than β cells and the glucagon content is much higher than that found in mammals.

Function. Before the association of diabetes mellitus with the pancreas was known, Bernard in 1877 observed that pancreatectomy in birds resulted in loss of weight and death.[17] It is of interest that Minkowski in 1893 found that this procedure did not induce glycosuria in the duck or pigeon.[48] Subsequently it was observed that partial pancreatectomy did lead to hyperglycaemia and glycosuria. The problem in birds is a loss of appetite and, if fed, they can survive for many months. If the pancreas is completely removed in the duck the blood glucose falls and this may result in convulsions, but on feeding the level rises and may reach hyperglycaemic levels. It would appear likely that the hypoglycaemia is due to the absence of glucagon, but after eating the lack of insulin is responsible for the elevation of the blood glucose. Glucagon administration will raise the blood glucose of both normal and pancreatectomized ducks, but hypophysectomy reduces the action of glucagon. Alloxan administration does not induce diabetes in ducks, owls, pigeons or domestic fowls. Only in the duck does this drug induce necrosis of the cells of the islets, and yet apparently there are no generalized ill effects.

In the domestic fowl removal of the pancreas is technically difficult and usually this organ is removed together with the duodenum. In the first few days the blood glucose rises, but then returns to normal. Unfortunately the animal only survives for a short time, as it dies from digestive disturbances following on the removal of the duodenum.

In some carnivorous birds—hawks, buzzards and ravens—diabetes mellitus is induced by pancreatectomy, but it is only transitory. In owls it has been reported that the diabetes is severe and in the great horned owl (*Bubo virginianus*) there is hyperglycaemia, ketonuria and loss of appetite, after pancreatectomy; the bird dies within a few days, insulin therapy being without effect.[35]

It would seem that in the non-carnivorous birds glucagon is an important factor in elevating the blood glucose and under these circumstances it is not surprising that the fasting level is relatively high, about 150 mg/100 ml; if glucagon is absent, there is hypoglycaemia. Birds are relatively resistant to the hypoglycaemic action of insulin. In fact the administration of commercial insulin results in an elevation of blood glucose, possibly because these preparations contain glucagon, although it is claimed that glucagon-free insulin still induces hyperglycaemia.

REPTILES

Histology. This is similar to the avian class in that the α cell is the predominant cell. In some of the snakes there is a spherical portion of the pancreas which consists mainly of the endocrine elements and these are referred to as principal islets.

Function. The fasting blood glucose in reptiles is between 50 and 200 mg/100 ml.[47] The metabolic changes induced by insulin are not seen for several days.

Pancreatectomy in the tortoise and turtle leads to hyperglycaemia, while insulin administration lowers the blood glucose; hypophysectomy only temporarily improves the diabetic condition. In the South American snake, *Xenodon merremi*, after pancreatectomy there is hypoglycaemia for a few days and then hyperglycaemia, but in lizards it would appear that this hypoglycaemia is permanent (cf. the duck). Further, with injections of commercial insulin the blood glucose rises and this response in lizards is the same as that observed in some non-carnivorous birds. Lizards are remarkably resistant to the hypoglycaemic action of insulin, even if pancreatectomized to remove the source of glucagon.

AMPHIBIANS

Histology. It is suggested that in newts and salamanders there are only β cells, whereas the frogs and toads probably possess both α and β cells, but basically the pattern is similar to other classes.

Function. In frogs and toads pancreatectomy results in diabetes mellitus, but in the summer months the diabetic condition sometimes improves, as there may be regeneration of remnants of islet tissue. The severity of the diabetes is increased by injection of extracts of the pars distalis, and lessened by hypophysectomy.

The absence of α cells in newts and salamanders may account for their low fasting blood glucose, which is between 15 and 30 mg/100 ml, their sensitivity to insulin and their resistance to glucagon which is a foreign factor to them. The fasting blood glucose in frogs and toads is higher, between 35 and 80 mg/100 ml.[47] Amphibians, like reptiles, do not respond to insulin for several days.

FISHES

As the function of the islet tissue in teleosts and elasmobranchs is essentially similar, they are considered together.

Histology. In teleosts the islet cells occur in clumps in the gall bladder, spleen, pylorus and caecum, whereas in elasmobranchs the islets are imbedded in the pancreas and consist of cells around the small ducts. Elasmobranchs and teleosts possess both α and β cells. The angler fish and the catfish have principal islets, as in some of the snakes.

Function. Preparations of islet tissue from elasmobranchs or teleosts, when injected into mammals, lower the blood glucose, but within their own group the effect is variable and less marked.

There are seasonal variations in the number of both the α and

β cells, and it is believed that the former secrete glucagon and the latter insulin. In the winter the α cells are more numerous, whereas in summer the β cells predominate.

The fasting blood glucose is very variable and probably ranges from 20 to 185 mg/100 ml.[47] Pancreatectomy in the eel leads to an inconstant glycosuria, but in selachians there may be marked hyperglycaemia following destruction of the β cells with alloxan. Hypophysectomy lowers the elevated blood glucose of the pancreatectomized dogfish (*Mustelus canis*).

CYCLOSTOMES

Anatomy and histology. In the wall, at the junction of the fore- and mid-gut, there are several cell masses which by staining techniques are found to differ from the β cells of the higher vertebrates; but, as glucose administration induces hyperactivity, it is likely that this tissue has the same physiological function as the islets of the higher vertebrates.

Function. Little is known of the function of these cell masses, but it would appear likely that insulin, or an insulin-like substance, is secreted, which aids glucose metabolism.

Summary

The principal hormone of the islet tissue of the pancreas of most vertebrates is insulin, and it is likely that all classes possess this hormone, which is necessary for the utilization of glucose by the tissues. There is general agreement that the β cells secrete insulin, but there is less certainty over the detailed histological appearance of the islet tissue in the vertebrate classes. The mammalian series has been the one most closely studied.

The capacity to elaborate insulin does exist in the embryo, but the time at which this occurs varies in different classes. Whether insulin secretion actually takes place in the embryo has not yet been settled.

Mammals vary in their response to alloxan; in some it causes destruction of the β cells, while others (for example guinea-pigs) are highly resistant to it. This drug has a destructive action on the islet cells of the duck, but there is still some dispute whether it has any effect on these cells in fishes.

Amphibians and mammals, in general, resist hyperglycaemia and the blood glucose level is relatively stable; whereas some fishes, reptiles and birds may have large fluctuations of hyperglycaemia, but hypoglycaemia is not easily induced; that is they are resistant to insulin.

Pancreatectomy leads to hyperglycaemia in mammals, carnivorous birds, amphibians, some reptiles and some fish. In ducks and lizards this procedure leads to a fall of blood glucose, probably because glucagon has an important function in elevating this level in these two vertebrates, unlike the mammals where its function is still uncertain. It is believed that glucagon may be absent in newts and salamanders.

Recently it has been suggested that insulin in the young mammal promotes growth and it appears likely that it acts synergistically with growth hormone; in the absence of insulin, growth hormone fails to induce protein anabolism.

8

Hormones of the alimentary canal and the placenta

HORMONES OF THE ALIMENTARY CANAL

THE precise origin of these hormones remains unknown and, unlike those previously discussed, the gastrointestinal hormones are independent of one another. Unfortunately little is known about the comparative endocrinology of this system and it has only been studied in a few of the mammals. These hormones have never been isolated in pure form, with the possible exception of secretin, but there is evidence that they are polypeptides.

1. *Gastrin*
It has been shown that the isolated denervated gastric mucosa will secrete hydrochloric acid when food is present in the main stomach; the chemical messenger concerned, gastrin, is released there in the presence of digesting protein. The richest source of gastrin is the pyloric region of the stomach which also contains histamine. Histamine will stimulate acid secretion by the stomach and there was some doubt whether gastrin was a separate substance. However, gastric extracts, which are believed to be histamine-free, are still able to stimulate the secretion of hydrochloric acid. Histaminase, which destroys histamine, does not affect the potency of the extract and gastrin appears to be a true hormone. A neuronal pathway is possibly involved in the release of gastrin, as the application of atropine inhibits its secretion.

2. *Enterogastrone*
The presence of fats or hypertonic sugar solutions in the duodenum results in the release of enterogastrone, which inhibits

both the secretion of hydrochloric acid and the motility of the stomach; the latter action is only observed if the vagal innervation of the stomach is intact. The hormone has little effect on the secretion of pepsin or mucus.

Evidence of the hormonal nature of enterogastrone is given by the fact that the presence of fats in the duodenum induces inhibition of secretion of hydrochloric acid by the denervated stomach. Fats injected intravenously do not affect gastric secretion, and thus the observed inhibition of gastric secretion cannot be due to the simple absorption of fats. The role of enterogastrone is probably to protect the gastric mucosa from the continued action of hydrochloric acid, after the digested food has left the stomach.

3. Secretin

This hormone is of considerable interest because of the classical experiments of Bayliss and Starling (1902),[14] who demonstrated for the first time the probable existence of chemical messengers. It was their experiments on secretin which started the scientific study of hormones. They showed that in the presence of hydrochloric acid, the duodenal mucosa released a substance into the blood stream which stimulated the exocrine secretion of the pancreas, that is the external secretion of a gland. It was established that the presence of hydrochloric acid in the denervated duodenum would cause the flow of pancreatic juices, whereas acid introduced directly into the blood stream had no action. Lastly it was demonstrated that if a neutral extract, prepared by treating the duodenal mucosa with the acid, was injected intravenously a pancreatic flow was initiated. The endocrine nature of the response was confirmed by the later observation that two dogs with a common vascular connection would both have pancreatic secretion, if hydrochloric acid was introduced into the duodenum of only one.[1]

It has been claimed that the active principle, secretin, has been isolated. Injection of this hormone only results in a flow of pancreatic fluid which is poor in enzyme content. Another substance named pancreozymin has been separated, and it induces a flow rich in enzymes. It may be that under normal conditions both secretin and pancreozymin are released together.

Hydrochloric acid is not the only substance which induces the secretion of secretin; both digesting fat and bile salts are effective. Hence human subjects, with the not uncommon condition of achlorhydria (absence of hydrochloric acid), still possess a humoral mechanism to initiate the flow of pancreatic enzymes. Another action of secretin is to stimulate the formation of bile salts by the liver. This may be another important action of the hormone, as bile salts play a significant role in digestion.

That secretin may be present in other vertebrates is suggested by the finding that an injection of mammalian secretin, or the presence of acid in the alimentary canal, will induce pancreatic flow in one genus (*Raja*) of elasmobranch fishes.

4. *Cholecystokinin*

A chemical messenger, cholecystokinin, so called because it causes contraction of the gall bladder, is released by the cells of the duodenal mucosa when they are in contact with fats or hydrochloric acid. This contraction results in the expulsion of bile, a necessary factor in the digestion of food. Denervation of the gall bladder does not inhibit the action of cholecystokinin. It has been demonstrated by cross-circulation experiments in dogs that this emptying of the gall bladder is achieved by a humoral mechanism.[3]

As discussed in Chapter 1, although it is accepted that specialized cells of the upper part of the alimentary canal secrete hormones, this tissue is not recognized as an endocrine gland.

THE PLACENTA

While viviparity may occur in poikilothermic vertebrates, and in some a structure develops which enables the embryo to be nourished by the transfer of food from the maternal blood, reference to the placenta in this discussion only applies to Eutherian mammals. Primarily the placenta, a very vascular organ, allows nutritive material and oxygen to diffuse from the mother to the foetus; waste products pass in the reverse direction. It must be emphasized that maternal blood never mixes with foetal.

In addition to these functions, there is indirect evidence that cells of the placenta derived from the embryo (trophoblasts) secrete hormones. It is believed that both oestradiol and progesterone are essential for the maintenance of pregnancy. In the early stages, spaying always results in the termination of pregnancy, but if this procedure is performed later, pregnancy continues in some mammals (cat, dog, monkey and man). Further, in the spayed pregnant woman, derivatives of oestradiol and progesterone are still excreted in the urine. It is assumed that the main source of these hormones is the placenta, the adrenal cortex only making a minor contribution. Oestrogens (mainly oestriol) and progesterone can be extracted from the placenta, but these hormones are not necessarily secreted by the placenta, as they could have been extracted by the placenta from the blood.

Pituitary gonadotrophins are required to maintain pregnancy, but hypophysectomy at the later stages does not lead to abortion in some mammals (mouse, rat, guinea-pig, monkey and man). Initially it is likely that pituitary gonadotrophins are necessary for the further development of the corpus luteum, enabling the rate of secretion of progesterone to rise. Subsequently the placenta secretes the necessary gonadotrophins and later still there is no need to maintain the corpus luteum, as progesterone is secreted by the placenta. This is the probable sequence of events in man. The evidence in favour of this view is that the excretion of gonadotrophin reaches its peak in the first month of pregnancy and falls fairly steeply by the fourth month. The excretory products of oestradiol and progesterone increase from the first month and continue to increase until birth. The high rate of excretion of gonadotrophins during the first month can be detected relatively simply; injection of the urine will induce ovulation in virgin rabbits, or spermiation in male toads (pregnancy tests).

Although the criteria described in Chapter 1 for establishing a tissue as an endocrine gland cannot be applied to the placenta, this organ appears to secrete hormones and may be regarded as an endocrine gland. The placental hormones assist the organism in maintaining pregnancy independently of maternal hormones.

9

Local hormones

THESE substances are produced locally and act in the vicinity of their production.

1. *Acetylcholine*

This highly important substance is released by the motor nerves and is responsible for the development of an end plate potential. The end plate is a specialized tissue on the surface of the muscle which is chemically excitable, and produces an electric potential which initiates muscular contraction. Acetylcholine is also released in the ganglia of the autonomic nerves and at the endings of the parasympathetic nerves, acting as a neurotransmitter substance; that is it transmits the impulses across the gap between the axons and the dendrites of nerve cells, or between the axon endings and the tissue. It is certain that acetylcholine alone is not responsible for synaptic transmission inside the central nervous system. Injections of acetylcholine induce the same changes as parasympathetic stimulation.

The autonomic nervous system consists of two parts—parasympathetic and sympathetic. These are responsible for the control of the vegetative systems of the organism; for example, the rate and strength of the heart-beat, the blood pressure, the propulsive movements of the alimentary canal (peristalsis), and in the homoiothermic vertebrates it regulates the temperature.

The classical experiments of Loewi (1921)[42] established that on stimulation of the vagus nerve a chemical substance is released from the endings in the frog's heart. Later this chemical substance was identified as acetylcholine. An enzyme (choline esterase), normally present in tissues and blood, rapidly destroys acetylcholine and thus the action of the local hormone is brief, unless it is continuously released.

The actions of acetylcholine can be summarized as those similar to a combination of muscarine and nicotine. The nicotinic actions of acetylcholine are exemplified by the transmitter action in the ganglia and at the end plates. The muscarinic actions are the slowing of the heart, increased peristalsis, gastric secretion, constriction of the bronchi, etc. Atropine only prevents the muscarinic action of acetylcholine.

2. *Noradrenaline*

This hormone, non-methylated adrenaline, is released from the nerve endings of the sympathetic nervous system and from the adrenal medulla. It is a powerful vasoconstrictor, and unlike adrenaline has virtually no vasodilator action. It is claimed that, compared to adrenaline, it has only a weak metabolic action; that is on the metabolic rate and the breakdown of tissue glycogen. Further, it only slightly increases the force of the cardiac contraction.

3. *Histamine*

Histamine is present in many of the tissues of the body, and it is a powerful vasodilator. There is a correlation between the number of mast cells and the concentration of histamine. While the mast cell is not the only source of this local hormone, it is an important one, as in injury it is the main supply of the hormone, and may be responsible for the associated vascular changes which occur. The release of histamine may also be responsible for many of the observed changes in allergy (for example nettlerash). The lining of the alimentary canal has a relatively high concentration of histamine and on administration it stimulates the gastric glands to secrete hydrochloric acid, but whether it plays any part in the control of gastric secretion is not known.

Many tissues contain histaminase, an enzyme that destroys histamine.

4. *5-Hydroxytryptamine*

Blood platelets contain this local hormone (5-HT), and when

blood clots the substance is released; it constricts small blood vessels. The vasoconstrictor substance present in the alimentary canal has been identified as 5-HT and, as it can act as a stimulator of peristalsis, it has been suggested that this may be its physiological action.

Chromaffin tissue not only contains adrenaline but also 5-HT. Cells in the alimentary canal which take up silver stain are referred to as argentaffin tissue and are rich sources of 5-HT. Tumours of the argentaffin tissue in man occur and large quantities of 5-HT are released leading to high blood pressure in the blood vessels of the lungs.

It has been found that, when an anti-metabolite of 5-HT, namely lysergic acid diethylamide, is administered to man, there are serious mental disturbances. It is doubtful whether one can deduce from this observation that 5-HT is essential for the normal function of the cerebral cortex. It is of interest to note that the plant-growth hormone auxin, which is indole-3-acetic acid, is closely related to 5-HT.

5. *Bradykinin*

Incubation of plasma with certain proteolytic enzymes (for example trypsin) results in the release of bradykinin which is a vasodilator substance. There is some evidence that actively secreting sweat glands may release an enzyme which acts on the substrate in the plasma to release bradykinin. This would induce local vasodilatation and the extra volume of blood is needed for the increased activity of the gland. Further, this vasodilatation is of the cutaneous vessels, and with an increased flow of blood to the skin there is a greater dissipation of heat from the body. This mechanism may contribute to the maintenance of body temperature, as the sweat glands are usually active in a hot environment.

10

Pigmentation, and organs which may be endocrine glands; notes on possible hormones

PIGMENTATION

IN GENERAL, pigmentation is utilized by the organism for protection—to conceal the animal by allowing it to merge with the background. In addition, it may be employed to indicate a state of sexual readiness, and it is possible that colour change could vary the heat exchanged with the external environment.

In the skin there are specialized cells, chromatophores, which carry the pigment, and they are black, yellow or red; these cells are named melanophores, xanthophores and erythrophores respectively. As most of the investigations have been carried out on melanophores, only these cells will be considered. Melanophores are found in all vertebrate classes, but only in the poikilothermic vertebrates is there continual movement of the pigment. In man, during intra-uterine development, cells called melanoblasts migrate from the neural crest of the central nervous system to the skin. These cells in the adult are referred to as melanocytes and in these cells melanin is synthesized. Under the influence of ultra-violet light the rate of synthesis increases. It is assumed that the melanophore of the lower vertebrates has a similar origin and is the homologue of the melanocyte.

In poikilothermic vertebrates changes of colour are induced by movement of the pigment inside the cell which has branching processes: the pigment is said to be concentrated or dispersed. Control of this pigment movement is either hormonal, nervous or possibly genetically determined. The hormone responsible for dispersion of the pigment is MSH (secreted by the pars intermedia, Chapter 2). It has been suggested that another hormone, not identified, causes concentration of the pigment and that the balance of these two hormones controls the colour, but this hypothesis has yet to be firmly established. It has been claimed that the adenohypophysis secretes the putative constrictor hormone, and recently the pineal has been implicated as the source of this substance. A serious difficulty in this type of investigation is that adrenaline causes concentration. This hormone is released during sympathetic activity, and puncture of the skin may be sufficient to excite the sympathetic system. Thus even the injection of an inert material may cause concentration of the melanin. There is no doubt that in the cold-blooded vertebrates MSH is a true hormone controlling the dispersion of the granules. This hormone alone could control the movement of the pigment granules and it is not necessary to assume the existence of a second concentrating hormone. Removal of the pars intermedia in amphibians, elasmobranch fish and some reptiles results in a permanent light skin colour. The hormone MSH not only acts on the melanophores, but also on the xanthophores and erythrophores. In addition, it promotes the formation of melanin and in the absence of the hormone the pigment content of the skin falls. As relatively impure preparations of the hormone have been used in the past, it is possible that MSH may consist of more than one hormone.

In reptiles only the group Lacertilia shows marked colour changes. In the chameleon the colour changes are remarkably varied and there is evidence that in this animal, unlike some other reptiles, colour control is effected by the nervous system.

Amphibians on a dark illuminated background darken in colour (pigment dispersed) and lighten in colour (pigment concentrated) if the background is light. The receptor organs for the response are the retinae of the eyes, and the effector mechanism is the rate of secretion of MSH; a high blood level of the hormone dispersing, and a low level concentrating, the pigment granules. The pars intermedia and the retina must be connected in some manner. There is little doubt that the described changes are dependent on this neuro-hormonal reflex and not on a direct nervous control of the melanophores. Destruction of either the afferent or efferent mechanisms abolishes the response. If the animals are blind, the changes are the same as observed in the young larvae: the skin lightens in darkness and darkens in bright light. This pigment movement is probably the direct effect of light on the melanophores.

As in amphibians, the elasmobranch skin colour is controlled by the level of MSH. The teleosts differ in that the melanophores are innervated and the pigment movement is under nervous control; the blood level of MSH may assist in the control of colour.

A characteristic feature of hormonally controlled melanophores is that colour change takes hours to occur, whereas this is achieved in minutes if there is nervous control. In brief the melanophores of the amphibians, elasmobranchs and some reptiles are controlled by the level of MSH. It is assumed that any stimulus which induces a colour change in these vertebrates is mediated by the hormone. Similarly in the chameleons and teleosts, whatever the stimulus to change skin colour, the effector mechanism is nervous. A more detailed account of the control of skin colour in poikilothermic vertebrates has been published.[1]

In birds, pigmentation of feathers is a complex problem and it is likely that the final picture is not solely dependent on a combination of hormones. Thyroxine in some species may favour pigmentation, while in others it causes lightening of colour. Undoubtedly the sex hormones make a real contribution, affecting the hue and colour distribution. In the weaver finch LH promotes melanin formation, and the adrenal cortical hormones may also play a part. Although it is true that there is no discrete pars intermedia in birds, it is possible to detect MSH activity in the pituitary gland. It is not possible, therefore, to exclude this hormone from playing some part in pigmentation.

The factors controlling pigmentation in man are unknown, but with the advent of pure preparations of MSH it has been possible to show that this hormone does cause darkening of the skin: one mechanism by which this is induced is increased melanin synthesis. There are some interesting observations made on pigmentation in diseases of man. In Addison's disease there is the characteristic darkening of the skin which is probably induced by an excess of ACTH. This hormone has similar actions to MSH on the melanocyte; this is not surprising in view of their structural similarity. The excess of ACTH is induced by the absence of adrenal cortical hormones.

A distressing condition called vitiligo, or leucodermia, may occur in man. Areas of skin lose their pigmentation and the skin around appears darker; this results in a mottled appearance. Little is known about the cause of this condition, but it may be seen in thyroid disorders or in syphilis or it may occur for no apparent reason, particularly in the elderly. Histological examination of the skin has revealed that there is impaired melanin synthesis in the melanocyte. Recently it has been found that administration of 8-methoxy-psoralen (isolated from *Ammi majus* and some other plants), topically and/or orally, is of benefit in about 25% of the patients.

ORGANS WHICH MAY BE
ENDOCRINE GLANDS

1. *Pineal*

This structure lies in the roof of the third ventricle. There is some evidence that the pineal complex of some lizards may have endocrine activity and may play a part in the register of solar radiations. It has been suggested that this complex controls the amount of movements made under different solar conditions, and therefore indirectly influences body temperature.

Recently it has been suggested that the pineal is the source of adrenoglomerulotrophin, a substance which stimulates the zona glomerulosa of the adrenal cortex to secrete aldosterone (Chapter 4). As pinealectomy only temporarily reduces aldosterone output, the organ can only be regarded as a possible store and is not the site of secretion. The whole subject requires careful investigation, as there may be significant differences between the various classes of vertebrates.

An entirely different substance called melatonin (a tryptamine derivative) has been isolated from the pineal. In very small doses

E

this will cause concentration of the melanophores of the frog's skin, but there is no evidence that this substance is a hormone.

In conclusion, therefore, the pineal is not accepted as an endocrine gland, except possibly in lizards.

2. *Thymus*

The history of the function of the thymus has had a fluctuating course, and it is still uncertain whether this tissue is an endocrine gland.

In man a disease called myasthenia gravis may be associated with a thymic tumour and, when this occurs, it is suggested that the tumour secretes an enzyme which inactivates acetylcholine (the neurotransmitter agent inducing muscular contraction). The patient suffers from a weakness which is only apparent after some movements have been made. Removal of the tumour is often of great therapeutic value. Accepting that thymic tumours do secrete this enzyme provides no evidence that the thymus is an endocrine gland. Diseased organs may secrete active substances which are not released under normal physiological circumstances. Finally, it must be emphasized that there are other causes of myasthenia gravis. Very recently it has been shown that in the immature animal, this gland may secrete a factor essential for the normal development of lymphocytes.

3. *Spleen*

At one time it appeared that the spleen secreted substances essential for the proper maturation of the erythrocyte. At present the organ is not regarded as an endocrine gland.

NOTES ON POSSIBLE HORMONES

1. *Angiotensin*

As discussed in Chapter 4, an enzyme, renin, is released from the kidneys when the blood flow is reduced, for example during a fall of blood pressure. This enzyme converts a protein, angiotensinogen, in the plasma to angiotensin. Angiotensin is a vasoconstrictor agent, and would therefore elevate the blood pressure. It is believed that this may be a mechanism whereby serious falls in the blood pressure are prevented. At one time it was suggested that excess angiotensin was the cause of hypertension (high blood pressure) in man, but this is not likely. It could well be responsible for the elevation of the blood pressure when one kidney is diseased. Angiotensin may control the secretion of aldosterone by the adrenal cortex (Chapter 4).

2. *Erythropoietin*

If there is a lack of oxygen in the blood, red cell production increases. There is some evidence that this stimulation may be due to erythropoietin, a humoral factor secreted by the kidney. At present there are still some doubts as to the existence and role of erythropoietin.

3. *Relaxin*

At parturition the pelvic ligaments relax, and it may be that a substance called relaxin, which it is claimed is secreted by the ovaries and/or the uterus, is responsible for this change. The evidence in favour of the hormonal nature of relaxin is poor.

4. *Adrenoglomerulotrophin*

The evidence in favour of this agent being a hormone is still in serious doubt. References to this have been made earlier in this chapter and in Chapter 4.

II

Endocrine systems in invertebrates

ANNELIDS

A VERY large proportion of the nerve cells in the supra-oesophageal ganglia of annelid worms show the morphological characteristics of gland cells and there are indications that some at least of these cells are engaged in endocrine function (p. 163). Numerous axonal pathways have been traced from certain glandular cells in the brain of the marine worm *Nephthys*, and it has been shown that the secretion of at least one of these cell groups (B-type cell in nucleus W) passes down axons to the base of the brain where the membranes investing it are specialized, and where the dorsal blood vessel, sometimes in the form of a plexus, is in intimate contact with the fibre terminations. It seems likely that hormonal material from neurosecretory cells may pass into the blood stream at this point, which morphologically resembles neurosecretory release centres in arthropods. There are also indications of other neurosecretory pathways, in particular the circum-oesophageal connectives along which neurosecretory material may pass.

Thus far neurosecretion appears to constitute the principal endocrine control in annelids, but this group has only recently received the adequate attention of endocrinologists and the possibilities of other forms of endocrine control have not been fully explored. Nor is it yet possible to distinguish with certainty by histological means those cells of the central nervous system engaged in neurosecretion from those which have purely nervous activity.

Evidence that the colour changes of crustaceans were evoked by hormones produced in their eyestalks (p. 146) led to a search for the endocrine tissue responsible for hormone production. In a series of studies on the nervous system, Hanström described two structures in the *eyestalk* which he thought might be secretory in function; one of these was the blood gland and the other was named the X organ (Fig. 8). It appeared that the blood gland was the more likely release centre as it lay in the wall of a blood sinus, and was thereby well placed for the release of hormones into the blood stream. It was therefore renamed the *sinus gland*, a name which has been retained.

Detailed accounts of early work on the sinus gland have been published, [21], [40] and it will suffice here to point out that the early investigators who studied this organ were impressed by its apparently complex innervation yet extreme simplicity of structure. A search for cytological detail revealed no clear cellular structure and by 1947, more than ten years after the identification of the sinus gland, J. B. Panouse was able to give but few details of its structure despite a painstaking histological study.

During the two decades, however, following the discovery of endocrine activity in crustaceans some workers had not been satisfied with the widely accepted view that the sinus gland was the only source of chromactivating hormones in crustaceans. A series of extraction and injection experiments indicated a portion of the central nervous system including the tritocerebral connectives and commissure as a potent source of chromactivating substances.

Eventually in 1951 two workers, engaged in independent but parallel studies, showed for the first time by combined histological and physiological studies that chromactivating hormones could be associated with secretory material lying within axons of central nervous system neurones. M. Enami, studying the crab *Sesarma*, showed a correlation between the chromactivating potency of extracts and cells with stainable material within the central nervous system and in particular demonstrated abundant secretory material within axons leading from groups of cells in the medulla terminalis in the eyestalk to the sinus gland (Fig. 8). Enami, however, still looked for normal endocrine activity in the sinus gland and suggested that the secretory material he observed might represent raw material for synthesis in the sinus gland. In the tritocerebral commissure region of the gulf shrimp *Penaeus braziliensis* a correlation between secretory material within axons and chromactivating potency of extracts was demonstrated and it was suggested that a process of neurosecretion takes place.[39]

During the past decade studies have made it abundantly clear that the greater part of the known endocrine activity in crustaceans is by neurosecretion. Many studies have shown that the sinus gland consists essentially of clusters of terminations of neurosecretory fibres which originate in cell groups in various parts of the eyestalk and also in the brain. The most noticeable of these cell groups is that described by Enami in the medulla terminalis, but the sinus gland also receives fibres from many other regions (see Fig. 8). At least six types of neurosecretory nerve endings may be recognized in the sinus gland of the blue crab *Callinectes sapidus*, and it seems likely that these may be derived from different groups of neurosecretory cells.

It is unfortunate that a number of American workers have used the term *X organ* to describe a group of neurosecretory cells in the medulla terminalis, for the name X organ was used by Hanström to describe an entirely different structure. This indiscriminate use of the term X organ has led to confusion and readers of the literature should take care to note whether, when the term X organ is used, the medulla terminalis X organ is intended or whether Hanström's X organ is the one described. Hanström's X organ appears to arise in evolution from a sensory pore in the more primitive crustaceans, and may therefore be termed the sensory pore X organ or SPX. It differs from the medulla terminalis X organ in a fundamental way, namely that it consists partly of the terminations of neurosecretory fibres whereas the medulla terminalis X organ is comprised entirely of the *perikarya* of neurosecretory elements. It is clearly necessary, when considering complex and diffuse neurosecretory systems

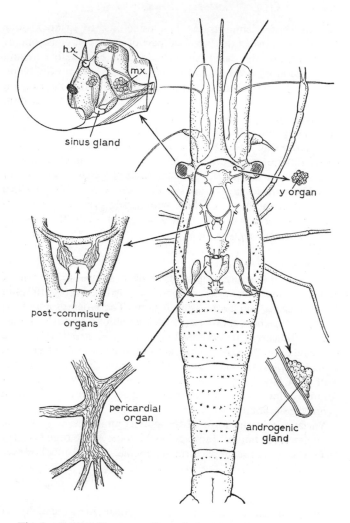

Fig. 8 A semi-diagrammatic representation of the endocrine tissues in a natantian decapod crustacean. On the left the three principal neurosecretory release centres are shown. On the right the y organ and androgenic gland. h.x. = Hanstrom's X organ m.x. = medulla terminalis X organ

such as those demonstrated in crustaceans, to make a clear distinction between the proximal part of a system, consisting of perikarya, and the distal part. The latter is essentially a region where secretory products are stored and released into the blood stream, whereas the proximal part is probably the main region of hormone synthesis. It has been suggested that the term *neurohaemal organ* might be employed to describe regions like the sinus gland which consist essentially of neurosecretory fibre terminations in association with the wall of a blood sinus.[40] Using this nomenclature, the principal neurohaemal organs of crustaceans so far described are the sinus glands and the sensory pore X organs in the eyestalks of those crustaceans with stalked eyes and in the heads of those with sessile eyes, and the post-commissure organs and the pericardial organs in the thoracic and abdominal regions (see Fig. 8).

Post-commissure organs

The post-commissure organs have been shown to consist of lamellar extensions of nerves containing neurosecretory fibres in the connective and commissure regions. These nerves appear to originate in the supra-oesophageal ganglion; methylene blue studies indicate a tritocerebral origin. In the primitive prawns (Penaeidae) each post-commissure organ has the form of a flat disc, 5 to 7μ in thickness and 150μ in diameter, attached to the wall of a blood sinus. This general form is very similar to a primitive sinus gland such as that described in some of the more primitive decapods.

Variations in the form of the post-commissure organs have been described but in all species in which they have been detected so far they have the simple form of lamellae, which differ however in position and shape.

Pericardial organs

A very similar system of lamellae consisting essentially of neurosecretory fibre terminations has been described as peri-cardial because the organs lie in the pericardium. These neuro-haemal organs were first described in *Squilla mantis* under the name of dorsal lamellae because in this species some lie free within the pericardium stretching from one side to the other, spanning the whole cavity. It was subsequently found, however, that the dorsal lamellae were but part of a diffuse system which also comprised neurohaemal organs spread over the wall of the pericardium, and that in crabs the greater part of the system lay on the inside of the lateral pericardial wall in such a position that their stoutest parts span the three openings of the branchio-pericardial veins. The name pericardial organ is now therefore given to the whole system of neurohaemal organs lying within the pericardium. Recently Maynard has given a very detailed and beautiful account of these organs in crabs.[45]

The Y organ

An endocrine gland, named the Y organ, has been described in 58 species of malacostracan crustaceans. Its cells, equal in size, have an average diameter of 10μ and are rich in ribonucleases and alkaline phosphatases. It lacks a secretory canal and is not especially vascularized except in crabs, in which it is relatively large, and receives innervation from the sub-oesophageal ganglion.

The Y organ is located in the antennary segment of those species which have a maxillary excretory organ, and in the second maxillary segment of those which have an antennary excretory organ. Experimental evidence (p. 159) has shown that the Y organ plays a part in the regulation of growth and moulting, and there are indications that this endocrine organ is the homologue of the ecdysial gland of insects and that their hormones may be chemically similar if not identical.

The androgenic gland

In all crustaceans studied so far except for certain isopods a gland, named the androgenic gland, is found near the subterminal region of the vas deferens, between the muscles of the coxopodite of the last thoracic leg. In newly formed parts of the gland the cells are usually linearly arranged. Later the cells increase in size, becoming multinucleated and vacuolated.

Finally the nuclei become pycnotic and the cells degenerate. The gland typically consists of a pyramidal mass of cells, about 250μ across the base; there is no obvious vascularization and no secretory duct. Experimental evidence (p. 166) indicates an endocrine function for the androgenic gland, which appears to control all the male sexual characters, primary as well as secondary.

INSECTS

The endocrine system of insects is in part neurosecretory. Groups of neurosecretory cells in the brain discharge their products along axons to a system of paired bodies, the *corpora cardiaca* and *corpora allata*, which lie in the head directly behind the brain (Fig. 9). These, and the *prothoracic* or *ecdysial glands* in the first segment of the thorax, comprise the endocrine system. There is some evidence that the main function of the neurosecretory system is the control of the remainder of the endocrine system.

The most conspicuous neurosecretory cells in the insect brain are those which lie in two clusters in the pars intercerebralis. In the silkworm *Cecropia* there are sixteen cells in this region, arranged in paired groups of eight cells each. In the moth *Mimas tiliæ* twenty cells are present.

In addition to the central mass of neurosecretory cells there are lateral groups also. In the Cecropia silkworm there are two lateral groups of five cells each. In the phasmid *Carausius morosus* similar lateral groups in each cerebral lobe contain five to six cells each; in this species a third group in the tritocerebral region on either side has been observed, and it has been shown recently that this group is present also in some other insect orders.

The brains of insect larvae appear to contain more neurosecretory cell groups than those of adults. Six groups of such cells have been observed in the brain of the larva of the blow fly *Lucilia caesar*.

The products of the neurosecretory cells in the brain pass along nerves, which have been described as *nervi corporis cardiaci*, to the corpora cardiaca. These nerve fibres, and their perikarya, are neurosecretory in the sense that they contain secretory products which stain by the Gomori and aldehyde fuchsin techniques.

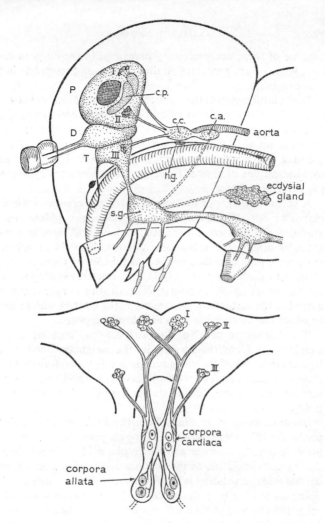

Fig. 9 Diagrams to show the general form and position of the endocrine tissues of insects, as seen from the left side (upper figure) and above (lower figure). The form of the retrocerebral complex differs in different insects (see text); these diagrams are more representative of the simpler orders of insects

I, II, III = neurosecretory cell groups   P = protocerebrum
D = deutocerebrum   T = tritocerebrum   c.p. = corpora pedunculata
c.c. = corpora cardiaca   c.a. = corpora allata   h.g. = hypocerebral ganglion   s.g. = sub-oesophageal ganglion

Some of these neurosecretory fibres end in the corpora cardiaca, while others pass through these bodies and terminate in the corpora allata.

The ventral region of the corpora cardiaca of *Carausius* consists essentially of neurosecretory fibres of the nervi corporis cardiaci. The largest endings, over 5μ in diameter, contain secretory granules up to 3,000 Å in diameter; other endings contain granules with a maximum diameter of 1,500 Å. There are therefore indications of at least two types of neurosecretory fibres in the corpora cardiaca.

A peripheral zone of the corpora cardiaca consists mainly of glandular cells. These contain an abundance of phloxinophilic granules. Electron microscope studies have indicated that these granules originate in close association with ovoid or spherical concentric multilamellate systems of tubules or cisternae in the cytoplasm, each approximately 1μ in diameter. Pseudopodia-like extensions of these glandular cells of the corpora cardiaca extend to the surface and apparently make contact with an aorta to which the corpora cardiaca are closely apposed.

The 'glandular cells' of the corpora cardiaca develop as evaginations from the foregut in the neighbourhood of the hypocerebral ganglion. It has been suggested therefore that these glandular cells may be modified nerve cells, and therefore in a sense neurosecretory; further studies are needed to elucidate this point.

Some neurosecretory fibres from the brain pass through the corpora cardiaca and terminate in the corpora allata. In the stick insect *Carausius morosus* and other phasmids a lumen formed during embryonic life, as the corpora allata arise from an ectodermal fold, persists and is lined by neurosecretory fibre terminations; these have been described as the nervi corporis allati. In other insect groups various forms of corpus allatum are found. Characteristically the corpus allatum is a single structure, without a lumen, and permeated by axons of the nervi corporis allati. Together the corpora cardiaca and corpus allatum constitute the *retrocerebral complex* and lie in close relation to the hypocerebral ganglion of the insect's stomodeal nervous system. An innervation from the sub-oesophageal ganglion is sometimes found. In some species the ecdysial glands also may become closely associated with the retrocerebral complex. An extreme of complexity is reached in dipteran insects which possess the so-called ring of Weismann around the aorta. This ring is in fact a complete endocrine complex which includes corpora cardiaca, corpora allata and ecdysial glands.

The ecdysial gland

This endocrine gland, first described in the eighteenth century, has been given many different names, which have depended on the final location of the gland. The structure originates from the ectoderm of the ventrocaudal part of the head and has been called the prothoracic, thoracic, peritracheal and ventral gland in different insects. Gorbman and Bern[3] have preferred the name ecdysial gland, since this tissue is the site of production of the hormone *ecdysone* (p. 161). The ecdysial gland is simple in structure, consisting of an unorganized mass of secretory cells, sometimes diffuse, with an abundant blood supply and innervation from the sub-oesophageal ganglion. It degenerates in most adult insects.

Cells of the neurosecretory system of the brain, those of the corpora cardiaca and those of the corpora allata pass through secretory cycles which are related to stages of development of the insect. During the diapause of *Mimas tiliae* the neurosecretory cells of the brain of the pupa are relatively small ($24-7\mu$) and no signs of secretion are found along their axons. If diapause is terminated by placing the pupae in a temperature of $3°C$ signs of active secretion appear; first globules and strands of basophilic material accumulate, followed by the appearance of acidophilic droplets which first nearly fill the cell and then pass along the axon, leaving large vacuoles in the cytoplasm of the perikaryon, which has by now increased in size to $27-32\mu$. Comparable changes in the brains of cockroaches and phasmids have also been described.

Cells of the corpora allata also show cyclic phases of secretion and multiplication during development. A new phase of activity starts after each moult is completed. A phase of mitotic activity is followed by an increase in size of some cells, some of which become polyploid and form giant cells. Granules appear in the larger cells, and accumulate in vacuoles which eventually come to lie outside the cells, in intercellular spaces.

The sub-oesophageal ganglion

Neurosecretory cells have been detected in the sub-oesophageal ganglion of some insects. In the Ephemeroptera and Plecoptera axons from these cells appear to make anatomical connections with the ecdysial gland. In the cockroach *Leucophaea* these cells present a variety of appearances in fixed preparations, and have been shown to alter after ovariectomy.

12

The endocrine control of effector systems in invertebrates

THE regulation of colour change, retinal pigment movements and heart-beat in crustaceans, and of colour change and heart-beat in insects, appears to be under endocrine control.

1 Colour change

CRUSTACEANS

The colour changes of crustaceans in relation to illumination and background have attracted the attention of investigators since they were first described in the prawn *Hippolyte* about a hundred years ago. The colour cells or chromatophores are exceptionally sensitive indicators of physiological change. In consequence experimental work seems generally to have been attended by results and the literature is embarrassingly voluminous for a reviewer who wishes to present a concise yet comprehensive account of chromactivating hormones. Many of the early experiments depended on injection procedures using crude extracts, and the results obtained were not always indicative of hormonal activity, though they were sometimes so interpreted.

The effectors for colour change, the chromatophores, are usually found directly underneath or within the hypodermis. They have many finely branched processes and may exist as single cells or form syncytia; those that are monochromatic seem to consist of a single cell. At one time it was thought that chromatophores were amoeboid cells, but it is now generally accepted that the branched processes are permanently fixed in position and that changes take place by the migration of pigment granules along these predetermined pathways (Fig. 10). When a pigment is fully dispersed it exerts its maximal effect on the colour of the animal. Conversely when it is retracted to a punctate spot in the centre of the chromatophore it has a minimal influence on colour.

Many natantian decapods have elaborate colour patterns, formed by the regular arrangement of polychromatic chromatophores. As an example we may select the common prawn *Leander serratus*, which has been chosen by many European research workers for physiological studies. Three main chromatophores are responsible for the colour pattern of this species.

(i) *Small red chromatophores* are diffusely distributed and form a general background colour; under the microscope each of these is seen to contain a red pigment and also a yellow pigment, each in separate branched processes.

(ii) *Large red chromatophores* are essentially the same as the small red chromatophores in appearance, but are much larger and are arranged in lines, forming dark bands of colour.

(iii) *White light-reflecting chromatophores* are regularly distributed, but widely dispersed. They contribute to the pattern and are especially noticeable when the animal is on a fairly dark background. Each contains red, yellow and white pigments.

The chromatophores, and indeed the pigments within them, show a complete independence. We may find individuals of all shades of colour and pattern in their natural environment, though the pigment of any one chromatophore type will be in synchrony with others of the same type.

Broadly considered, polychromatic chromatophores such as those described in the prawn *Leander serratus* are characteristic of the decapod Natantia, while monochromatic or bichromatic chromatophores are characteristic of Astacura, Anomura, Brachyura, Isopoda and Stomatopoda.

Crustacean chromatophores show three main types of response to environment.

(a) *A response to total illumination.* Normally the stronger the illumination the greater degree of dispersal of the chromatophore

pigments, whether in light-absorbing or light-reflecting chromatophores. Experimental results indicate that this is a direct
response of the chromatophore to change of illumination. If a
small portion of the leg of the crab *Uca* is shielded but the rest of
the animal is illuminated, dispersal of the black pigment takes
place in the illuminated portion, but not in the shielded area. It
is possible, of course, that such differences might have a hormonal
basis, if illumination were sensitizing the chromatophores to a
hormone activating them.[40]

Comparative injection experiments in *Uca* in light and darkness
indicate that illumination augments the action of the injected
material on the chromatophores causing greater dispersal.

(b) *Response to temperature.* If the temperature is raised above
the normal range to which a crustacean is accustomed, white
pigments are dispersed and red pigments are concentrated. The
result is that, at these higher temperatures, the body reflects more,
and absorbs less, radiant energy. This response, therefore, seems
to act as a body-temperature-regulating mechanism. Barrington
has suggested that in some cases the heat-regulating significance
of chromatophore changes may be greater than their importance
in concealment.[1] There is no direct evidence that the response of
chromatophores to temperature change has an endocrine basis.

(c) *An albedo response.* This, a background response, renders
the animals inconspicuous by matching the body colour with the
shade of the background. Typically the dark light-absorbing
pigments disperse and the pale light-reflecting pigments con-
centrate when the animal is on an illuminated black background.
The pigments assume the opposite condition on an illuminated
white background.

It is necessary to distinguish between such a physiological
background response, brought about by the redistribution of
pigment within chromatophores, and morphological changes
brought about by formation or destruction of pigment. If a
crustacean is kept, for example, on an illuminated red background for weeks the amount of red pigment in the chromatophores will increase.

The exact part played by hormones in morphological pigment
changes has not yet been ascertained, but there is evidence that

the physiological background responses are under hormonal control.

The state of the chromatophore pigments in a crustacean at any one moment is compounded of a number of distinct responses, namely to (a) total illumination, (b) the ratio of incident illumination to that reflected from the background, (c) the wavelength of incident and reflected light, and (d) temperature. These reactions in turn are superimposed on fundamental rhythms of colour change in synchrony with solar and lunar rhythms (see page 155.) Most of these responses seem to be under endocrine control.

The first convincing demonstration of endocrine control in crustaceans was given by E. B. Perkins working on the prawn *Palaemonetes*, and G. Koller studying the shrimp *Crangon*. These authors independently showed that transection of nerves did not affect the state of chromatophore pigments, but that interruption of the blood supply was followed by an immobility of pigments in chromatophores nearby. These early experiments pointed to the probability of a pigment-concentrating hormone, originating in the eyestalks, and the possibility of a pigment-dispersing hormone, formed in the rostral region. Some investigators, however, did not consider that the evidence for pigment-dispersing hormones was adequate, and during the first decade following the discovery of endocrine control of colour change in crustaceans attempts were made to explain the differential movements of pigment in chromatophores on the basis of a single hormone acting at different threshold values. Later evidence favoured several distinct hormones.

Removal of the eyes and eyestalks leads to a darkening of shrimps and prawns, but to a paling in crabs. Moreover, it was shown that extracts which dispersed dark pigments in the fiddler crab *Uca* concentrated dark pigments of the shrimp *Palaemonetes*, and later reciprocal injection experiments and differential solubility analyses showed that when extracts from a number of different crustaceans were compared a fraction of eyestalk extract soluble in 100% ethyl alcohol had a predominantly 'Palaemonetes-concentrating' effect, whereas the residue after alcohol extraction had mainly a 'Uca-dispersing' effect.

During the 1940s methods of differential solubility were used to separate chromactivating hormones. Eyestalks of the shrimp *Crangon* were extracted in alcohol. Such an alcohol-soluble fraction when injected into eyeless animals concentrated the black chromatophores of the body, but was without effect on those of the telson and of the uropods. On the other hand, a water extraction of the alcohol-insoluble residue resulted in an extract which concentrated the dark chromatophores of both the body and the tail.

Similar methods applied to the tritocerebral commissure region (p. 136) gave an alcohol-soluble body-lightening hormone, and an alcohol-insoluble fraction which darkened both the body and the tail. By about 1953 it became apparent that a number of chromactivating hormones were being produced in the crustacean central nervous system by a process of neurosecretion and a more precise localization of hormone-producing areas became possible, but methods for the purification of crude extracts had not yet been developed.

One general difficulty which confronts students of invertebrate endocrinology is the problem of isolation and identification of hormones from minute quantities of material, since the endocrine organs are invariably small. In order to overcome this difficulty the method of paper electrophoresis was used to separate chromactivating hormones in *Leander serratus*,[41] and this method has subsequently been used by other investigators. By means of this technique an abundant, stable and active substance was found in a number of neurosecretory tissues in crustaceans and was termed the *A-substance*. It disappeared slowly from extracts which were allowed to stand for some hours at room temperature (boiling prevented this) but retained activity for months or even years in a dried form; and its activity could be destroyed by treatment with a trypsin extract.

The A-substance, with these properties and with specific effects on the chromatophores of *Leander*, was found in the sinus glands and post-commissure organs of *Leander* and in *corpora cardiaca* of the stick insect *Carausius* and of the silkworm *Bombyx*. It was soluble in pure methanol and it seems highly probable that the A-substance corresponds to the alcohol-soluble fractions of the eyestalks of *Crangon*. It had a very strong effect on the large red and the small red chromatophores of *Leander*, concentrating their pigments.

It now seems highly probable that the A-substance was the active pigment-concentrating principle in the crude extracts used in early experiments on crustacean colour change.

The post-commissure organs of *Leander* yielded a substance which was termed the *B-substance*. This resembled the A-substance in its relative immobility in electrophoresis and in its inability to pass through cellophane membranes, but unlike the A-substance it was electronegative at pH 7·8. It was relatively unstable and disappeared rapidly from extracts allowed to stand at room temperature. Like the A-substance it concentrated the large red chromatophores of *Leander* but dispersed pigment in the small red chromatophores.

The method of separation by electrophoresis revealed yet another chromactivating substance, named the *A'-substance*, which lay close to the position of the A-substance under the conditions of electrophoresis used. Like the A-substance and the B-substance, it concentrated red pigments in the large red chromatophores of *Leander*, but unlike the A-substance it concentrated white pigments.

It is interesting to note that all the three substances, A, A' and B, had similar effects on the large red chromatophores of *Leander* but different effects on other chromatophore types. It seems possible that the molecules of different chromactivating hormones in crustaceans may bear a general basic resemblance but differ in detail. The A-, A'- and B-substances did not readily pass through dialysis membranes, and we may consider therefore whether these substances are more likely to be the active chromactivating hormones or precursor substances. If *Leander* extracts were boiled before paper electrophoresis, only the A-, A'- and B-substances referred to above were detected. If, however, unboiled extracts were used, at least two additional distinct chromactivating substances, but with smaller molecules, were detected. If extracts were allowed to stand at room temperature these *alpha substances*, as they were called, increased in amount as the A-substance decreased; there are some grounds therefore for the belief that these substances may be formed from the A-substance by enzymatic degradation. Possibly they may be closely related to the active hormones in the blood. After electrical stimulation of post-commissure organs of *Leander*, alpha substances were found in the surrounding fluid.

There is not space here to consider in detail the full range of chromactivating substances which have been indicated by experimental data. This is given elsewhere.[21, 40]

To summarize, it seems likely that each type of chromatophore pigment in crustaceans is affected by a distinct hormone, and that probably the movement of each pigment is regulated by a pair of antagonistic hormones, one effecting pigment-dispersal and the other pigment-concentration. Thus far there are indications that some at least of the chromactivating substances may be peptides.

Undoubtedly the sinus glands and the post-commissure organs are two most important neurohaemal organs for the release of chromactivating hormones, but one must not ignore the possibility that there may be other release centres for these hormones. Certainly extracts with chromactivating potency have been made from most parts of the crustacean central nervous system, and a correlation between the activity of many of these extracts and cells containing demonstrable secretory material has been made and has indicated that though neurosecretory axons from many of these cells terminate in the sinus-gland and post-commissure organs, it is possible also that some of them discharge their contained hormones elsewhere.

INSECTS

Most insects do not change colour in response to alterations of illumination or background. The phasmids or stick insects are an exception to this rule and their colour change has been extensively studied. The stick insect *Carausius morosus* darkens under the action of a hormone secreted by cells in the tritocerebral region; animals deprived of their brains remain permanently pale. The presence of an intact sub-oesophageal ganglion also appears to be necessary for the normal dark condition of the insect. There are indications that the chromactivating hormone, which promotes a redistribution of pigment in the hypodermis, not in specialized chromatophores, may pass from the tritocerebrum along the connectives and be released at the sub-oesophageal ganglion.

A brain hormone which promotes colour change in phasmids appears to be chemically different from the A-substance that effects crustacean colour change, although the A-substance is present in abundance in the corpora cardiaca of phasmids.

2 Retinal pigment movements

The eye of an arthropod consists of a number of distinct units called ommatidia, each comprising a lens system, pigment cells and a group of light-sensitive elements. The amount of light which reaches these photosensitive elements is regulated by movements of pigment. Some at least of these pigment movements are under endocrine control in crustaceans; the mechanism of control of similar pigment movements in insect eyes has not yet been ascertained.

The eye of *Leander serratus*, the common British prawn, is typical of the more advanced crustacean eye, in which there are three mobile pigments, generally known as the distal pigment, the proximal pigment and the reflecting pigment. In some of the more primitive prawns (for example some members of the *Penaeidae*), the distal and reflecting pigments are fixed in position, but the proximal pigment moves.

The eye of *Leander* consists of some 9,000 ommatidia, each of which has the structure shown in Fig. 10d. (p. 151). Light entering an ommatidium passes first through a slightly biconvex cornea, then through a crystalline cone, and finally impinges on a rhabdome, which is surrounded by retinular cells. Each rhabdome is cone-shaped and appears under the optical microscope to consist of a number of superimposed discs. Under the electron microscope these are resolved into fine extensions of the retinular cells.

Each ommatidium contains eight retinular cells, but one of these is very reduced in size. Proximally these sense-cells taper to fibres which pass through the basement membrane and gather to form the lamina ganglionaris. A dark light-absorbing pigment, probably ommatin, lies in the retinular cells and screens the

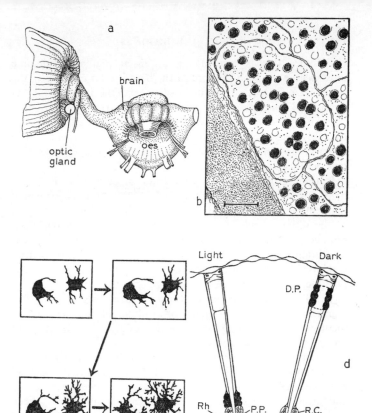

Fig. 10 (a) The brain and optic ganglia of a cephalopod mollusc (Argonauta). The optic gland, suspected of endocrine function, is shown. oes = oesophagus

(b) A small portion of a pericardial organ redrawn from an electron micrograph. Some fibre terminals, lying just below the surface, containing neurosecretory inclusions, are shown. (The scale line is one micron)

(c) Successive stages in the expansion of two chromatophores, redrawn from photographs

(d) Two ommatidia of a crustacean eye, one in a light-adapted condition, the other in a dark-adapted state. D.P. = distal pigment P.P. = proximal pigment R.P. = reflecting pigment R.C. = retinular cell Rh = rhabdome

rhabdome; this is termed the proximal pigment. In some crustacean eyes, such as those of the hermit crab *Eupagurus*, the proximal pigment is fixed in position and the image is of the apposition type in which each rhabdome receives only that illumination which has passed through its own cornea and cone. In many crustaceans, however, movements of pigment permit either an apposition image or a superposition image, depending on conditions of illumination.

In the eye of *Leander* an apposition image is given in bright light, for under such conditions of illumination the proximal pigment lies above the basement membrane in the distal region of the retinular cells. Under dim illumination or in darkness, however, the proximal pigment migrates below the basement membrane and a superposition image, in which illumination reaching a rhabdome may pass through several ommatidia, is possible. Fig. 10 shows the two extreme positions of the proximal pigment and moreover illustrates the movements of the distal pigment under differing conditions of illumination. These movements also contribute to the conversion of a superposition eye to an apposition eye and vice versa.

A number of workers have investigated the possibility that the movements of the proximal pigment are under endocrine control, but their results have been inconclusive. The evidence for endocrine control of the proximal pigment has recently been reviewed; it appears that, though there is insufficient evidence to enable us to show with confidence that movements of the proximal retinal pigment are not under endocrine control, such data as we have do not favour this possibility.[40]

There is abundant evidence, on the other hand, that movements of the distal retinal pigment and the reflecting pigment are under endocrine control. The first indication of this was given by L. H. Kleinholz who brought about typical light-adaptation of the distal and reflecting pigments in individuals of *Palaemonetes vulgaris* kept in darkness by injecting them with an eyestalk extract; the degree of migration of the distal pigment was proportional to the dose.

Recently, in an attempt to localize the source of the 'light-adapting' distal retinal pigment hormone, Kleinholz and his collaborators have assayed various extracts in a number of species, and find considerable diversity. Extracts of the sinus glands of *Pandalus borealis* contained a light-adapting hormone for the distal pigment, but so also did extracts of the eyestalks from which the sinus glands had been removed. Eyestalks of the lobster, *Homarus*, and of certain brachyuran crustaceans had little distal retinal pigment activity.

To sum up, it seems likely that in some species at least the sinus glands are not the terminal organs where the light-adapting hormones for distal retinal pigment are stored and released; the neurohaemal organ involved in the release of the distal pigment light-adapting hormone in these species has not yet been determined.

There is some evidence that the movements of the distal retinal pigment may be regulated by antagonistic light-adapting and dark-adapting hormones. The distal retinal pigment can take up positions intermediate between those of light-adaptation and dark-adaptation, depending on conditions of illumination and the shade of the background on which a shrimp is placed.

Both light-adapting and dark-adapting hormones were found to be heat-stable, inactivated by trypsin, and to migrate in an electric field. On the basis of these observations it has been suggested that they may be polypeptides.

Electrophoresis studies indicated an isoelectric point close to pH 9·0 for the dark-adapting hormone and one higher than pH 9·0 for the light-adapting hormone affecting the retinal pigments. It is interesting to compare these figures with results obtained from chromactivating hormones. These were only slightly mobile at a pH of 7·6, indicating that this was close to their isoelectric points.[41]

Injection experiments have further indicated a distinction between retinal pigment hormones and chromactivating hormones. Purified extracts with great effect on chromatophore pigments (e.g. the A-substance) can be injected into *Leander* kept in darkness without apparently affecting the position of their distal retinal pigments.

The reflecting pigment is contained in cells with the general form of white chromatophores, which spread over the basement membrane between the clusters of retinular cells. Extracts which affect the white chromatophores of the integument also affect the reflecting pigment cells of the eye. There is, however, insufficient evidence as yet to decide whether more than one hormone is involved. The retinal pigments in the eyes of insects move in response to intensity of illumination. There is, however, no evidence that these pigment movements are under hormonal control.

3 Heart-beat

Substances with effects on the frequency and amplitude of the heart-beat have been extracted from the sinus glands and pericardial organs of crustaceans and from the corpora cardiaca of insects. Thus far, however, the evidence for heart-regulating hormones depends on injection experiments only, without corresponding ablation experiments, and we do not know to what extent the regulation of the heart-beat under normal environmental conditions is dependent on hormonal control.

In 1937 Welsh indicated that a heart-accelerating extract could be obtained from the sinus glands of *Palaemonetes* and showed that conditions of illumination and background which brought about chromatophore concentration also evoked an increase in the rate of heart-beat. More recent work suggests, however, that the heart-affecting substances are distinct from the chromactivating substances in sinus glands. The evidence for heart-regulating substances in sinus glands was suggestive, but, since the extracts were tested in whole animals and not on isolated hearts, the possibility that these extracts acted not on the heart but evoked release of heart-regulating substances from some endocrine tissue could not be excluded. There is more reason to believe that the *pericardial organs* of crustaceans are of predominant importance in the regulation of the heart-beat.

The identification of the pericardial organs as an endocrine complex provides an exception to the general rule (p. 171), that in invertebrate endocrinology physiology precedes anatomy, for it was suggested by Alexandrowicz, on purely anatomical evidence, that the organs which he described might have an endocrine function; subsequently Alexandrowicz and Carlisle[10] demonstrated the pharmacological effect of pericardial organ extracts, added to fluid perfusing isolated hearts.

Administration of a pericardial organ extract was followed in most cases by a marked increase in the frequency and amplitude of the heart-beat, but a certain unevenness of response could be detected; sometimes the frequency was increased, but not the amplitude, giving rise to a suspicion that more than one heart-stimulating substance might be implicated.

D. B. Carlisle has advanced the view that an ortho-dihydroxytryptamine was responsible for some of the effects of pericardial organ extracts on the heart-beat. J. H. Welsh and D. M. Maynard have subsequently showed that a substance with polypeptide characteristics was abundant in pericardial organ extracts, and could be shown to affect the rate of heart-beat. They indicated also an unexpectedly high concentration of 5-hydroxytryptamine in the pericardial organs of the species they studied, but could not confirm the proposition of Carlisle that the main active principle was an ortho-dihydroxytryptamine.

Electron-microscope studies on the pericardial organs of the Mediterranean crustacean *Squilla mantis* have shown neurosecretory fibres of two types and also intrinsic cells containing secretory droplets. It cannot be assumed that these elements are all engaged in the endocrine regulation of the heart-beat, but it seems likely that more than one hormone may be implicated in cardiac control. Possibly rapid and transitory alterations in the heart-beat may be mediated by a catecholamine while more prolonged control is effected by a peptide hormone.

4 Rhythms

Pigment movements in the eyes and chromatophores of crustaceans, known to be under endocrine control, show persistent diurnal rhythms, which are to some degree independent of the environment. A detailed discussion of these rhythms is beyond the scope of this book and they will only be considered here in so far as they relate to general endocrine control.

F. A. Brown and his collaborators have made a long series

of investigations on the colour changes of the fiddler crab *Uca pugnax*, in which three chromatophore pigments are involved: red, white and black. These pigments, under endocrine control, move in synchrony with solar (24 hr) and lunar (tidal) cycles, and such rhythms persist even though the animals may be kept under constant illumination or in darkness. The exact position of the chromatophore pigments seems to depend therefore on internal as well as external factors.

When *Uca* is in its normal habitat the position of the red pigment is usually dependent on the shade of the background, and this response takes precedence over the underlying diurnal rhythm.

Retinal pigments of crustaceans also show 24 hr rhythms of migration which persist in constant darkness or, more rarely, under illumination.

Persistent rhythms of locomotor activity have been demonstrated in many insects, especially members of the Orthoptera. Janet Harker has carried out a series of experiments which indicate that endocrine activity is implicated in these rhythms, by means of a hormone which promotes activity. Since an activity rhythm can be relayed from one cockroach to another joined to it in paraboisis, it has been postulated than an endocrine secretion released from the sub-oesophageal ganglion is an intermediary in the production of the rhythm. It is also possible to produce a normal rhythm of activity in headless cockroaches by implanting the sub-oesophageal ganglia taken from normally rhythmic cockroaches. The rhythm of the headless cockroach then follows the same rhythm as that which the donor was previously following, thus indicating an inherent rhythm of secretion in the sub-oesophageal ganglion. It has recently been found that injection of extracts of the sub-oesophageal ganglia into headless cockroaches does not give the same effect at all times in the 24 hours. Injections given in the evening are followed by more prolonged activity than occurs after morning injections. These results indicate that not only may there be regular rhythms of hormone production but possibly also rhythm of sensitivity of the target organs.

Studies on endocrine-controlled rhythms have a general

importance inasmuch as they show that hormone production and tissue sensitivity are not necessarily the same at all stages in a 24 hr cycle. This factor should be borne in mind when reading the literature and comparing the results given by different workers who may perhaps have carried out their experiments at different times of day, especially in the case of sensitive and ephemeral changes such as pigment movements.

13

The endocrine regulation
of metabolism and development
in invertebrates

EVIDENCE for the endocrine control of metabolism and development in annelids has been provided by studies on the regeneration of lost segments in marine polychaete worms under different conditions of experimentation.

If ragworms of the genus *Nereis* are deprived of a number of their posterior segments and are also decerebrated shortly before or after the loss of the segments a failure to regenerate these segments is observed. Yet such decerebrated animals can be stimulated to regenerate if a supra-oesophageal ganglion from another worm be implanted in their coelom, provided that this implanted brain is taken from a worm which has had a number of segments amputated about three days previously. If, however, the implanted brain is taken from a normal animal, or one in which amputation of segments has occurred four or five days previously, it seems unable to stimulate regeneration.

R. B. Clark has interpreted these results as an indication that after the posterior end of a nereid worm is amputated, a hormone accumulates in the supra-oesophageal ganglion, reaches a maximum on the third day, and is released into the circulation on the fourth day. The precise nature and action of this hormone have yet to be determined. There are some indications that the active principle is distinct from the so-called 'juvenile hormone' (p. 163) which appears to restrain the development of adult characteristics.

Moulting in crustaceans is evidently under endocrine control, for eyestalk removal is generally followed by an acceleration of moulting and it has been shown that this effect can be checked by implantation of the X-organ sinus-gland complex.

It seems likely, however, that endocrine activity in the eyestalk may not affect moulting directly, but through the endocrine activity of the Y organ (p. 137). A moulting hormone secreted by this structure is at present assumed to be similar if not identical to insect *ecdysone* which is known to promote moulting in insects.

The bulk of the evidence favours the existence of a hormone, produced in the X-organ sinus-gland neurosecretory system, which inhibits the activity of the Y organ. There are indications, however, that an antagonistic hormone, promoting Y-organ activity, may also be present in the eyestalk of some crustaceans. In the Mediterranean shrimp *Lysmata*, for example, a moult-accelerating substance can be extracted from the two X organs but not from the sinus gland. It has moreover been shown that eyestalk removal promotes moulting in the prawns (*Leander serratus*) at the French marine research station at Roscoff but the same operation inhibits moulting in prawns of the same species taken at Plymouth or Naples.

A possible explanation of these apparently contradictory results is that moulting is under the control of two distinct endocrine processes, one a direct restraint exerted by some substance in the eyestalk, acting directly on the tissues, and the other a moult-accelerating substance, produced by the Y organ, the activity of which is promoted by an eyestalk hormone. This explanation would bring the endocrine control of development in crustaceans and insects into line, for insect development seems to be regulated by a moult-promoting hormone released under trophic (that is excitatory) neurosecretory control and a juvenile hormone whose effects are, in a sense, antagonistic to the moult-promoting hormone, since it restrains the development of the tissues.

It is important to recognize, however, that moulting and

development are complex processes which involve many inter-
acting metabolic and morphological events. The picture of
possible endocrine control presented here is a simplified one. It
is possible that many hormones, affecting different phases of
moulting and development, may be involved. For a fuller account
the reader is referred to reviews of this subject.[3]

INSECTS

The post-embryonic development of insects is under endocrine
control. The first suggestion that this might be so was advanced
by Kopeč, who found that removal of the brain from young
caterpillars of the moth *Lymantria* suppressed pupation. Subsequent experimental work has shown that not only the
brain but also the retrocerebral complex (p. 139) are concerned
in the development of insects.[3, 65]

Growth and differentiation are synchronized in the normal
development of an insect. Each larval stage of pterygote insects
is distinct, separated from preceding and succeeding stages by
moults, or ecdyses. During a larval stage a new exoskeletal
integument is formed beneath the skin, which is cast off at the
moult. In the hetermetabolous insects (e.g. the tropical bug
Rhodnius) change in form during development is gradual and each
larval stage, known as a nymph, does not differ very greatly from
preceding and succeeding stages. In the holometabolous insects
(e.g. *Cecropia* moth) on the other hand a very radical change
takes place during pupation resulting in the destruction of larval
tissues and the construction of the adult insect. Sometimes the
pupal stage includes a period of quiescence, during which development is checked and the pupa remains dormant.

Moulting may therefore be regarded as the termination of a
phase of developmental activity, during which certain poten-
tialities of the cells of the body are realized, and not as a process
distinct from differentiation. The present theory of endocrine
control of insect development suggests that a hormone, named
ecdysone, favours growth and differentiation of adult structures
and is also responsible for the initiation of moulting and the
termination of diapause. In contrast another hormone, the

juvenile hormone or *neotenin*, appears to favour the growth and differentiation of larval structures. Normal development depends on changes in the relative amounts of ecdysone and the juvenile hormone which are available to the tissues. V. B. Wigglesworth has considered the action of the two hormones in terms of balanced interaction. Thus he suggests larval differentiation of a cell might occur in the presence of approximately equal amounts of ecdysone and neotenin; the pupal stage might occur in the presence of ecdysone and small amounts of neotenin, the adult condition would result from the action of ecdysone alone. Moulting would occur as the level of neotenin decreases towards the end of a larval stage and thus the level of ecdysone relative to neotenin becomes relatively high.

Ecdysone was first isolated and purified from extracts of the prothoracic or ecdysial glands by A. Butenandt and P. Karlson. Extracts derived from 500 kg of pupae of the silkworm *Bombyx mori* yielded two specific substances, α and β ecdysone, of which the former appeared to have the greater activity. The empirical formula has been given as $C_{18}H_{30}O_4$, but as yet the structural formula has not been determined, except for the presence of two rings in the molecule.

Some theories have been put forward to account for the action of ecdysone. C. M. Williams found that the tissues of the pupal cecropia moth are cyanide-insensitive and that this is due to a deficiency in cytochrome c. He has suggested therefore that one role of ecdysone may be to promote synthesis of this cytochrome. Karlson has suggested that ecdysone affects tyrosine metabolism and that this amino acid is eventually converted into N-acetyl dopamine, which plays a part in the sclerotization of the cuticle. It has been shown that after ecdysone injection a rise of Dopa decarboxylase activity and also of some components of the phenol oxidase system can be detected. Effects of ecdysone injections have been detected at the genetic level. Karlson has demonstrated that specific 'puffing' of bands on chromosomes can be elicited in the salivary glands of the midge *Chironomus* by injections of ecdysone and that puffs characteristic of the normal chromosomes of later larvae or prepupae could be evoked in earlier larvae in a matter of 15 to 30 min by low doses of ecdysone;

F

as little as $2 \cdot 10^{-6}$ μg ecdysone produced an effect. According to Karlson's concept the action of ecdysone may be to provoke activity of certain genes and so the production of specific enzymes which will in turn promote chemical syntheses leading to differentiation.

Secretion of ecdysone is in turn controlled by a trophic hormone which originates in the neurosecretory cell groups in the brain (see p. 138) and is secreted either directly into the blood by these cell-bodies or passed along neurosecretory axons to the corpora cardiaca and secreted there. Some evidence suggests that both medial and lateral cell groups are concerned.

It is interesting to note that neurosecretion by combining features of nervous and endocrine control permits a regulation of endocrine glands in relation to external stimuli. In *Rhodnius* the moult is initiated by abdominal distension after a blood meal; it is suggested that the recurrent nerve which proceeds anteriorly from the gut stimulates the neurosecretory centres of the brain to release their hormone and thereby promote secretion of ecdysone by the ecdysial glands. Williams found that chilling of the kind that the cecropia moth normally encounters during diapause potentiated the neurosecretory cells of the brain which thereafter could release their hormone.

Development of the adult characters of an insect is restrained by the activity of the corpora allata which produce the juvenile hormone or neotenin. Removal of the corpora allata from a larva or nymph results in premature moulting and the early attainment of an adult-like condition. Conversely the implantation of corpora allata can cause supernumerary moults and so prolong larval life. The juvenile hormone has not yet been extracted in a pure form and its molecular structure is not yet known.

14

The endocrine control of reproduction in invertebrates

ANNELIDS

IT IS possible to remove the 'brain' or supra-oesophageal ganglion from annelid worms without killing the operated animals. After extirpation of the brain from certain young marine worms (nereid and nephtyid polychaetes) somatic changes which normally are only found in sexually mature worms make their appearance. Histolysis of the musculature, development of new chaetae, enlargement of parapodial lamellae and development of the gametes are among the adult features which may be induced in young worms by brain extirpation. All these changes may be prevented by the implantation of the brain from an immature worm into a decerebrate animal. It is moreover possible to delay the onset of maturity in a normal worm by the implantation of an immature brain. These results have led to the suggestion that the supra-oesophageal ganglion of polychaete worms secretes a 'juvenile hormone' which restrains sexual maturation of both the germ plasm and the soma.

The endocrine control of sexual maturity in the terricolous oligochaete worms appears to differ from that of the marine polychaetes, for in the oligochaetes some hormonal factor originating in the supra-oesophageal ganglion appears to stimulate the appearance of somatic sexual characteristics. The histological appearance of certain cells in the brain varies with the seasons; an apparent draining off of secretory material occurs at the beginning of spring when the somatic sexual characteristics

163

are developing. There is as yet no clear indication that the development of the gametes in terricolous oligochaetes is regulated by 'brain hormones'.

It is, however, not easy to separate oogenesis from metamorphosis in annelid worms, for both processes may occur concurrently and make considerable metabolic demands on the animal, and there is always the possibility of interaction between the two processes. It is therefore difficult to establish experimentally whether one or two hormones may control metamorphosis and gametogenesis. Certainly both phenomena seem to be affected by secretions of the brain and occur in synchrony. The present evidence favours the possibility that one hormone, the 'juvenile hormone', restrains both gametogenesis and metamorphosis in polychaete worms, though the presence of some brain factor seems to be necessary for vitellogenesis once this has begun. A brain hormone seems to promote somatic maturation in oligo-chaete worms, but as yet there has been no convincing demonstration of endocrine control of gametogenesis in this group.

CRUSTACEANS

A number of endocrine tissues seem to be implicated in the regulation of sexual development in crustaceans. The present picture is a slightly confused one but the most likely hypothesis is that which suggests that the Y organ exerts a non-specific effect on the development of the gonads (as part of its general influence on development), that the androgenic gland exerts specific effects on primary and secondary sexual differentiation, and that the activities of both these endocrine glands are regulated by trophic hormones originating in the eyestalk. Some of the experimental evidence for this hypothesis will be summarized below.

A removal of the eyestalk from immature female crustaceans results in a rapid and considerable increase in the size of the ovary, and to premature oviposition in some species. The removal of the sinus glands alone is less effective than removal of the whole eyestalks and some investigators believed that some ovarian inhibiting factor might lie outside the sinus gland. It must be remembered however that the sinus gland is but a release centre for hormones produced elsewhere in the eyestalk (see p. 135). Injections of whole eyestalk extracts, or of sinus-gland extracts, or of extracts of the medulla terminalis X organ, have all proved effective in restraining the normal increase in ovarian size which precedes the breeding season in normal female crustaceans. These results have been taken as evidence for the existence of an ovarian inhibiting hormone in the X-organ sinus-gland complex.

The problem of whether an ovarian inhibiting hormone acts directly on the gonads or via some endocrine centre has not yet been solved with certainty, though there are indications of a direct effect in natantian decapods in which the ovarian inhibiting effect of the eyestalks appears to be sexually specific; that is, removal of the eyestalks is without effect on the male gonad. It is noteworthy however that in crabs the testis also is under inhibitory control, for removal of eyestalks in these animals leads to testis hypertrophy.

An ovarian inhibiting effect of crustacean eyestalk extracts was found when these were fed to honey-bees, and conversely the 'queen-substance' which is responsible for the suppression of the development of the ovaries of worker bees prevented ovarian proliferation when injected into eyestalkless *Leander*.

The Y organ seems also to play a part in the endocrine control of gonad development in crustaceans, for its ablation in either sex in crabs before the onset of sexual maturity leads to a considerable retardation of gametogenesis and to degenerative changes in the gonads. It is not yet clear however to what extent this effect is specific, for the Y organ is known to exert a general effect on metabolism, stimulating growth and differentiation, and it is possible that the gonadal anomalies in immature animals deprived of their Y organs may be a particular aspect of a more general effect.

In addition to the eyestalks and Y organ, yet another endocrine tissue, known as the androgenic gland (see p. 137), seems to be implicated in primary sexual differentiation. This organ, found in the male malacostracan crustacean, will, if implanted into a female in certain species (for example Amphipods), lead to the transformation of the ovary into a testis. Some crustaceans (for example Lysmata) undergo sex-reversal at a certain age, but it is not yet known whether the androgenic gland is involved in these changes.

The androgenic gland also exerts a hormonal influence on the secondary sexual characters in certain crustaceans. Its presence is necessary for the normal development of the male characters, including the sperm duct. In the female the sinus gland exerts an indirect effect by restraining the influence of the ovary, which appears to determine female characters. Transplantation of an ovary into a normal male is without effect on the secondary sex characters, but a similar operation performed on an androgenic gland-free male induced female characteristics.

It is evident, when the results reported above are examined, that the endocrine control of reproduction in crustaceans results from the integration of a number of endocrine tissues. We may recognize certain probable sequences of events.

Primary sexual differentiation in female crustaceans (and in the male brachyuran crustacean) appears to be regulated in the first place by some endocrine secretion, or secretions, originating in the eyestalk. It seems possible that this endocrine influence may exert at least some of its effects via the Y organ. Certainly the presence of a Y organ is necessary for the normal development of the gonads. Although, when the gonads are mature, ablation of the Y organ has no effect on them, removal of the eyestalks in mature crustaceans at a time when the animals are not breeding does lead to increase in size of the ovary. It has been suggested that the Y organ elaborates a specific hormone which is needed for the maturation of the gonad, but which is not necessary for the functioning of the gonad when this is ripe, but this suggestion has not yet received experimental confirmation.

There are indications that the androgenic gland plays an important part in primary and secondary sexual differentiation, and also some evidence that the eyestalk neurosecretory systems may influence the secretion of the androgenic gland.

There is some evidence that sexual maturity of the octopus is under endocrine control.[64] Maturation of the gonads in both sexes is related to the size and activity of two small bodies, each approximately 1 mm in diameter, which lie on the optic stalks and have been named the optic glands (Fig. 10). They consist of secretory cells and supporting cells, between which large numbers of nerve fibres ramify; they have also an abundant blood supply, and so have the normal attributes of an endocrine tissue.

The nerve supply to the optic glands, which originates in the subpedunculate dorsal lobe area, appears to inhibit their activity. Following nerve section, or removal of certain parts of the supra-oesophageal lobes, the denervated optic glands enlarge, and vacuoles appear in the cytoplasm of the secretory cells. Enlargement of the optic glands is always accompanied by considerable enlargement of the gonads (from one-five-hundredth of the body weight in the female to one-fifth of the body weight within five weeks of the operation; in males the testis enlarges by 50%). Wells and Wells interpret these results as implying an endocrine control of gonad maturation by a gonad-stimulating hormone, the secretion of which is regulated by inhibitory innervation from the higher optic centres of the brain; there is no evidence as yet to indicate a corresponding excitatory influence on the optic glands. Removal of the optic glands from adult animals did not result in any significant changes. The ovaries of operated animals kept for periods of up to seven weeks did not alter significantly although slight regression of the testis was observed in male operated animals kept for the same period.

It is not yet known whether removal of the optic glands from an immature animal would prevent normal sexual maturity, or whether precocious maturity could be provoked by injections of optic gland extract. Thus far therefore the evidence for endocrine control of gonad maturation in the octopus is largely by inference from the effects of interference with the nervous system. The experimental work, however, indicates the probability that the maturation of the gonads of the octopus, as in annelids, arthropods and vertebrates, is under endocrine control and that this in turn may be regulated by photoperiod via the optic centres.

15

General considerations

Neurosecretion

HORMONES have been defined as organic compounds, which are synthesized by specialized tissues (eg. the endocrine glands) and released to circulate in the blood stream; each has a particular effect—excitatory or inhibitory—on a particular tissue, the target organ. Evidence that a tissue is an endocrine gland is usually established by certain criteria though sometimes a direct proof may be difficult (see p. 12). The criteria used are not easy to apply to invertebrate animals. In some of these the blood system is very simple; the small size of the endocrine tissues makes ablation difficult and the collection of sufficient material for chemical analysis presents many problems.

Moreover, much of the endocrine activity in invertebrate animals is brought about by neurosecretion, in which elements of the nervous system do not subserve the more usual function of innervating muscles or exocrine glands, but instead synthesize considerable quantities of hormones which they store and release either into the blood stream or locally to excite or inhibit other endocrine tissues (p. 159). Many of these neurosecretory systems in invertebrates are diffuse and consequently the criteria of classical endocrinology, namely ablation and replacement therapy, are difficult if not impossible to apply. A similar situation occurs with the main neurosecretory system (the hypothalamus) of vertebrate animals. This structure is so situated and of such a form that total ablation is difficult; experiments on these neurosecretory systems have usually been limited to severing the tracts, or to electrical stimulation of the centres containing their cell-bodies.

In this book neurosecretion is considered as a special form of endocrine activity, but it would be prudent to recognize that neurosecretion does not fall precisely within the definition of endocrine systems as given at the beginning of this chapter and elsewhere (Chapter 1).

It is not easy to delimit precisely the field of endocrinology and separate it from the related method of control in the body, namely the nervous system. We have seen in this book that while some tissues, such as the thyroid, are specialized solely for the secretion of blood-borne hormones, others, for example the neurohypophysis, contain elements which serve a dual function, nervous and secretory. Moreover, some neurosecretory fibres may enter endocrine tissue, and directly influence its activity; for example, the pars intermedia of many vertebrates and some structures of the adenohypophysis of teleost fishes.

It is also difficult to delimit precisely the field of neurosecretion, for in fact secretion is an essential function of all nerves. For example, the endings of normal motor neurones liberate acetylcholine, and this seems to be contained before release in small vesicles, the synaptic vesicles. The difference between such neurones and neurosecretory neurones may be said to depend on the following criteria: (1) A characteristic neurosecretory neurone contains considerable quantities of secretory material contained in vesicles ranging in size from approximately 1,000 Ångstroms to 2,500 Ångstroms in diameter. (2) Thus far, methods of chemical analysis indicate that the characteristic neurosecretory product is peptide in nature. (3) Neurosecretory neurones do not appear to innervate muscles or exocrine glands, but either terminate in close proximity to the blood stream, or in some close spatial relationship with other endocrine tissues. These three criteria, taken together, may be used to define a certain class of nerves, which includes those which form the greater part of the neurohypophysis of vertebrate animals and the corpora cardiaca, sinus gland, post-commissure organs and other neurohaemal organs in invertebrates. Their functions appear to be either (a) endocrine, by the production and release of blood-borne hormones, or (b) neuroendocrine by a control of more orthodox endocrine tissues. They are therefore included in this book as an integral part of the endocrine system.

Endocrinology of invertebrates

For many years invertebrate endocrinology lagged behind vertebrate endocrinology, mainly owing to two causes. First, the lack of any apparent clinical significance in the studies on invertebrate endocrines. Secondly, the paucity of knowledge of the detailed anatomy of invertebrates when measured against the many centuries of careful studies on the anatomy of man. We find in fact when we survey the history of endocrinology that this study in vertebrates and invertebrates differs in one important respect, namely that many endocrine organs of vertebrates were described before their function was known, whereas hormonal actions were detected in many invertebrates before the associated endocrine tissues had been discovered.

In the early days of invertebrate endocrinology, attempts were made to obtain effects by injecting extracts of vertebrate endocrine organs into invertebrates and vice versa. Effects were obtained, and interpreted as indicating biochemical and functional similarities in the endocrine systems of different phyla. More recently, however, workers who have repeated such experiments, using more purified extracts, have failed to adduce convincing proof that hormones in different phyla are biochemically identical. It seems more likely that the results which were obtained in early injection experiments were due to either (a) a non-specific stress response to alien proteins, (b) a stimulation of the animal's own endocrine system by the injected material or (c) a non-specific response by the target system to the injected material. Chromatophores for instance are extremely sensitive indicators of physiological change and will respond to a wide variety of agents. Nevertheless, clear instances of endocrine control have been demonstrated in some invertebrate groups, notably the annelids and arthropods, and it is interesting to note that many of the activities under endocrine control in vertebrate animals (for example, colour change, development, reproductive maturation and behaviour) are also under endocrine control in invertebrates. This fact has tempted some writers to try and classify

endocrine systems on the basis of function.[5] Such an approach
has a certain usefulness, but if the definition of neurosecretion,
already given (p. 170), is accepted, then a great deal of invertebrate
hormone control is determined by this mechanism; whereas in
the vertebrates, if the hypothalamo-hypophysial system is
excluded, it is of minor importance.

Studies in the endocrinology of annelids and arthropods
indicate that neurosecretion is a more important form of
endocrine control in these groups than in vertebrates. Neurosecretion combines features of nervous and endocrine control.
The fact that nervous elements are employed, having synaptic
connections with other parts of the nervous system, means that
the relationship between the internal endocrine milieu and the
stimuli of the environment is a close one. The storage of hormonal material at nerve endings makes possible not only a fairly
rapid stimulation of a target organ but also prolonged stimulation without fatigue of the activating system. Such a system
is in fact well suited to an environment like the seas, the home
of so many invertebrates, in which slow rhythmical changes
due to the seasons and the tides are superimposed on more
rapid changes of environment due to movement by the animal.

The study of comparative endocrinology suggests that endocrine control may have arisen in the first place by specializa-
tion of certain elements of the nervous system to control 'long-
term' processes such as development, and also such functions as
colour change in which slow rhythmical changes and sudden
modifications are both important.

The chemistry and mode of action of hormones

Endocrinology was founded on extraction and injection experiments. Some of these involved experiments using different
species; for example extracts of sheep thyroid were used to
accelerate metamorphosis in tadpoles. The success of this and
similar early experiments raised hopes that relatively few
chemical compounds might bring about the various endocrine
effects observed in different species. It seemed possible that the
same hormones might be manufactured in the pituitary, thyroid
and other endocrine organs throughout the vertebrate series.

A more detailed knowledge of the biochemistry of hormones and of their action now permits a clearer understanding of the differences between the hormones of different species and makes it possible to discern certain general principles, namely (1) hormones with similar action even in related species, for example ox and pig, may nevertheless have a different chemical constitution; (2) extracts containing hormones may have either similar effects, or different effects if injected into members of different species; (3) the tissues of one species may be insensitive to a hormone which has an effect in another, even a related species. We may illustrate these generalizations by specific examples.

The vertebrate melanocyte-stimulating hormone (MSH) has received the attention of biochemists on account of the ease of obtaining suitable amounts of this hormone from meat-packing firms for analysis and the sensitivity of a biological test, using amphibian melanophores. Biochemical analysis has shown that substances with similar effects but different chemical constitution may be obtained from mammals of different species. The α MSH in the pituitary gland of pigs is, for example, chemically different from that in the pituitary of oxen (p. 23), yet both have similar effects on amphibian chromatophores. It is however possible to recognize a basic grouping of amino acids which is common to both forms of MSH, and it seems likely that this constitutes that part of the molecule which is active on chromatophores. Additional support for this view is provided by the fact that adrenocorticotrophin, another but distinct pituitary hormone, has a slight melanocyte-stimulating activity (about 1% or less). It is interesting to note that the basic sequence of amino acids found in all MSH preparations, from different species, namely methionine—glutamine—histidine—phenylalanine—arginine—tryptophane—glycine, is also present in the molecule of ACTH, and no doubt accounts for its slight melanocyte-stimulating activity.

In contrast to the similar hormonal action of dissimilar chemical compounds, we find that there are instances of a hormone having different effects in different species. For example attention has already been drawn to the action of luteotrophic hormone on water drive in amphibians. The pituitary glands of mammals contain abundant MSH yet these animals lack a pigmentary effector system. It has been suggested that MSH in these instances may be concerned in pigmentation by melanogens or in the facilitation of scotopic vision. A somewhat similar anomaly is found in arthropods in respect of chromatophore-activating hormones. A substance which brings about pigment movements in certain crustacean chromatophores is present in considerable amounts in the corpora cardiaca of insects (see p. 150), yet insects do not have chromatophores and we do not yet know the reason for the presence of this substance.

It is possible that a substance which acts as a hormone in one group of animals may be present, but not have a hormonal action, in another group due to tissue insensitivity. For instance, pituitary and thyroid hormones accelerate metamorphosis in certain amphibians but not in others. Frog tadpoles will change into adult frogs if given extracts of sheep thyroids; the axolotl, which does not normally metamorphose in its normal habitat, may be induced to do so by the administration of pituitary or thyroid extracts; yet *Necturus*, another urodele amphibian which does not metamorphose, cannot be made to do so by hormone injections. Yet another amphibian (*Eurycea tynerensis*)) will only partially metamorphose, even in concentrations of 10^{-6} thyroxine. It is evident that a wide range of tissue-sensitivity to thyroxine exists within the class Amphibia. Yet, are we justified in assuming that because a hormone does not promote a specific and expected action in an animal it may not be present in that animal subserving some other function?

The thyroid gland first makes its appearance in the phylogenetic series in the lamprey, being present in the larva as a mucus-secreting gland, the endostyle, which becomes transformed during metamorphosis into a typical follicular thyroid. Attempts to promote premature metamorphosis by treatment with thyroid or pituitary preparations have been unsuccessful, yet it can be shown that the endostyle is able to metabolize iodine and is responsive to extracts of mammalian thyroid-stimulating hormone. Observations such as those indicate that an endocrine tissue and hormone may be present in the phylogenetic series before a tissue-responsiveness to the hormone has evolved. For instance, the thyroid hormone acts on the basic metabolic rate of the homoiothermic birds and mammals but not on the basal metabolic rate of the poikilothermic fishes, amphibians and reptiles.

Yet it is clear, on the available evidence, that thyroxine plays an important part in the regulation of metabolic activity in poikilothermic forms. The deposition of guanine in the scales of fishes may be promoted by thyroid treatment. Such a silvering of scales is a normal event in the transformation of the parr to the smolt stage in the salmon, and this is accompanied by hypertrophy of the thyroid. Metamorphosis in amphibia is dependant on normal thyroid function. It is tempting in view of the wide distribution of thyroxine in the vertebrates to assign to it an influence on cell metabolism at some very elementary level; but is this view consistent with the specificity of thyroid action? Perhaps the answer will be found in a greater understanding of the influence of hormones on enzyme action. There are indications that thyroxine plays some part in phosphorylation by inhibiting or stimulating succinic dehydrogenase or succinoxidase activities, and moreover that in different tissues these activities behave somewhat selectively towards thyroxine and other thyroid hormones.

Our knowledge of the mode of action of hormones is incomplete. There are indications that hormones may influence gene action, enzyme action and the properties of membranes, and it is not easy to decide on which a hormone may have its primary action since these three constituents of cells are so closely related. For example, it has been shown that thyroxine causes mitochondria to swell, but it has been suggested that this may be accompanied by a spatial rearrangement of enzymes in the mitochondrial membranes and that it is this which causes disturbances in phosphorylation.

We have seen that in insects there is some evidence which points to a direct effect of a hormone on gene action (p. 161). Possibly hormones which affect rates of development may have their primary effect on genes, while others with more immediate effects (for example on chromatophores, muscles) may exert a primary effect on membranes or enzymes.

The identification of hormone-producing tissues

Ablation and replacement therapy may point to a tissue as the source of a number of hormones (for example the adenohypophysis). How then are we to decide whether certain cells manufacture particular hormones or whether a single cell type may produce more than one hormone? Sometimes this may be shown by changes in particular cells following removal of a target organ (for example the identification of gonadotrophins following castration). Removal of a target organ does, however, often seriously disturb the whole endocrine balance of the body and interpretation of its effects on endocrine tissues may be difficult.

Classification of different cell types by histological and histochemical reactions has also been attempted. It must be recognized, however, that this method, used alone, has certain dangers. For example, cells which stain differently may not represent different cell types, but a single type at different stages in a secretory cycle. The matter is further complicated by the fact that we have as yet no sure method, using optical microscopy, for deciding whether an endocrine cell is actively manufacturing a hormone, although sometimes indications of activity may be seen (for example basophilia, acid phosphatase activity). In the early days of endocrinology it was assumed that cells filled with secretory material were in the process of active manufacture and secretion. It is now recognized, however, that a cell in which the process of hormone release is proportionately as great or greater than the process of hormone manufacture could appear devoid of all secretory material although in fact it might be in a stage of intense activity. Thus a chromophobe cell might be one either in a state of quiescence or in a state of extreme activity: further evidence than that provided by histology alone might be required to decide between these two possibilities.

Hormones in blood

Much of the early experimental work in endocrinology was carried out using crude fractions of endocrine tissues; these were injected and the effects recorded. With the refinement of biochemical techniques, purer, and sometimes crystalline, forms of hormones were obtained. Such purification led to a greater clarity of experimental procedure and of the interpretation of results while at the same time presenting a new problem—were the active substances prepared by biochemical techniques identical with the hormones circulating in the blood stream?

It is difficult to obtain direct evidence on the state of hormones in the blood by isolating trace elements of these hormones; the methods used must be extremely sensitive yet, at the same time, specific and precise. As with the use of other biochemical methods of analysis, direct assay methods may alter the normal state of the hormone. For example, various indirect methods of observation have shown that insulin may circulate in the blood either in an active or 'unbound' state, or bound to some macromolecule which affects its physiochemical, biological or immunological properties. Indeed it seems probable that steroid hormones, thyroxine, catecholamines and many other hormones may all circulate in the blood in association with other substances. Direct methods of analysis might alter such complexes.

The evidence at present available does not enable us to decide in each case whether the association of hormones with macro-molecules in the blood serves as a means of transporting these hormones from the tissue of their origin to a target organ, or whether the primary significance of the association is to 'bind' the hormone and make it biologically inactive. Observations on insulin have indicated that a proportion of the hormone may circulate in an inactive state and part in an active condition, and that the relative amounts may depend on the general metabolic state of the individual. For example, in the fasting state insulin circulates in the blood of normal human beings mainly as a biologically inactive complex. A rise in the amount of glucose in the blood results in an increase in the biologically active form of insulin and a decrease in the concentration of the insulin com-plexes. It has been suggested that the disease diabetes mellitus may result not only from a lack of insulin in the blood but could result from the failure of the mechanism by which the balance of active and inactive insulin in the blood is regulated.

It is clear that any experimental investigation into an endocrine effect should take into account the general metabolic state of an individual. We have already seen that hormone production and tissue-sensitivity in some arthropod animals fluctuate rhythmically in synchrony with day and night, the tides or the seasons. It is evident therefore that two independent investigators studying an endocrine effect might arrive at different conclusions yet each might be correct if the metabolic state of their experimental animals, the time of day and the time of year were taken into account. This point should be borne in mind when assessing the sometimes conflicting evidence for endocrine effects. The endocrine system exists in a state of balance, not only between its constituent parts but also with the rest of the metabolic activities of the body and in some cases with the external environment as well.

Neuroendocrine relationships

We have seen that oestrogens stimulate nest-building activity in birds. We have seen also that the secretion of oestrogens is controlled by a pituitary hormone. In turn many secretions of the adenohypophysial gland appear to be mediated by the hypothalamus which itself receives sensory input from external and internal receptors. Through such a chain of controlling mechanisms external factors such as light influence sexual behaviour in birds and some other animals. Many instances of reproductive behaviour influenced by hormones may be given, in both vertebrates and invertebrates. Injections of luteotrophic hormone cause certain fishes to build nests, some birds to develop broody behaviour, and the rat and various other mammals to show maternal behaviour. The increased water drive of young salamanders induced by luteotrophic hormone, referred to elsewhere in this book (p. 27), has also some bearing on the study of reproductive behaviour since the eggs and early stages of development of salamanders require water.

The relationship between the central nervous system and the endocrine system is of major importance, yet the means by which the hypothalamus affects pituitary secretion is still a matter of controversy. It has been shown[32] that electrical stimulation of certain clearly definable areas of the hypothalamus can influence the secretions of thyroid, adrenal cortex, and gonad-stimulating hormones from the adenohypophysis, though direct electrical stimulation of the adenohypophysis did not result in trophic hormone secretion. A considerable body of evidence supports the view that the control of the adenohypophysis is not by direct innervation by motor fibres but rather by some form of neuro-secretion. The adenohypophysis homologue of fishes is, in some species, permeated by neurosecretory fibres and in the sea-horse, *Hippocampus*, some terminals of neurosecretory fibres have been shown to invest gonadotrophic cells. There is less evidence of direct innervation of the adenohypophysis by neurosecretory fibres in higher vertebrates, though these have been detected in the pars intermedia. The existence of a portal blood supply from the median eminence to the adenohypophysis does, however, provide a pathway along which hormones could pass from the neurosecretory fibres of the hypothalamus to the adeno-hypophysis to influence its secretion.

Such a conception of neurosecretory control of normal endocrine functions is supported by indirect evidence that in the invertebrates the regulation of the Y organ, the ecdysial glands and the corpora allata seem to be under neurosecretory control.

These and other studies emphasize the complexity of the endocrine system in an animal. It is likely that neurosecretory hormones may regulate the activity of other endocrine tissues, including probably the adenohypophysis. Evidently secretions of the adenohypophysis regulate the thyroid, adrenal cortex and other endocrine tissues. Furthermore there exists in many cases a delicate balance between the activity of a target organ and its controlling endocrine mechanism. It is not surprising that endocrinology is a complex subject which cannot easily be expressed in simple chemical and physical terms.

Bibliographical references

GENERAL READING

1 Barrington, E. J. W., 1963. *An introduction to general and comparative endocrinology.* Oxford Univ. Press

2 Best, C. H. and Taylor, N. B., 1961. *The physiological basis of medical practice; a text in applied physiology.* 7th ed., London

3 Gorbman, A. and Bern, H. A., 1962. *A textbook of comparative endocrinology.* New York

4 Hoar, W. S., 1957. Endocrine organs. In *The physiology of fishes,* edited by M. E. Brown, vol. 1. Metabolism. New York and London

5 Jenkins, P. M., 1962. *Animal hormones.* New York

6 Jones, I. C., 1957. *The adrenal cortex.* Cambridge Univ. Press

7 Noble, G. K., 1931. *The biology of the Amphibia.* (1954 reprint) New York

SPECIAL REFERENCES

8 Addison, T., 1868. *A collection of the published writings of Thomas Addison,* edited by Dr Wilks and Dr Daldy. London

9 Albright, F. and Reifenstein, E. C., 1948. *The parathyroid glands and metabolic bone disease; selected studies.* Baltimore

10 Alexandrowicz, J. S. and Carlisle, D. B., 1953. *J. mar. biol. Ass. U.K.,* 32, 175–92

11 Aristotle (a) *De Generatione Animalium.* V.7, 787 b.20 (b) *Historia Animalium.* IX. 50

12 Aschner, B., 1912. *Pflügers Arch. ges. Physiol.,* 146, 1–146

13 Banting, F. G. and Best, C. H., 1922. *J. Lab. clin. Med.*, 7, 251–66

14 Bayliss, W. M. and Starling, E. H., 1902. *J. Physiol., Lond.*, *28*, 325–53

15 Bell, G. H., Davidson, J. N. and Scarborough, H., 1961. *Textbook of physiology and biochemistry*. 5th ed., Edinburgh and London

16 Bernard, C., 1855. In *History of medicine*, 4th edition, 1929, F. H. Garrison, 544. Philadelphia and London

17 Bernard, C., 1877. Quoted in reference 35

18 Berthold, A. A., 1849. *Arch. Anat. Physiol.*, 42

19 Brown-Séquard, C. E. and d'Arsonval, A., 1891. *Arch. de Physiol.*, 5th series, III, 491–506
Brown-Séquard, C. E., 1889: *Lancet*, *2*, 105–7

20 Caldeyro-Barcia, R. and Poseiro, J. J., 1959. *Ann. N.Y. Acad. Sci.*, *75*, 813–30

21 Carlisle, D. B. and Knowles, F. G. W., 1959. *Endocrine control in crustaceans*. Cambridge Univ. Press

22 Collip, J. B., 1925. *J. biol. Chem.*, *63*, 395–438

23 Cowie, A. T. and Folley, S. J., 1957. In *The Neurohypophysis*, ed. H. Heller, pp. 183–201, being the Proceedings of the 8th symposium of the Colston Research Society held in the University of Bristol, 9–12 April 1956. London

24 Dale, H. H., 1906. *J. Physiol. Lond.*, *34*, 163–206.

25 De Meyer, J., 1909. *Arch. Fisiol.*, 7, 96–9

26 Dioscorides, P. de Simplicidus. II. 96

27 Evans, H. M. and Long, J. A., 1922. *Proc. Nat. Acad. Sci.*, *8*, 38–9

28 Fisher, C., Ingram, W. B. and Ranson, S. W., 1938. *Diabetes insipidus and the neuro-hormonal control of water balance.* Michigan

29 Frazer, J. F. D., 1961. *The sexual cycle of vertebrates*. London

30 Greep, R. O. and Talmage, R. V., 1961. *The parathyroids*. Proceedings of a Symposium on advances in parathyroid research held at the Rice Institute, Houston, Texas

31 Harms, J. W., 1929. *Z. wiss. Zool.. Abt. A.*, *133*, 211–397

32 Harris, G. W., 1955. *Neural control of the pituitary gland*. (Monographs of the Physiological Society no. 3) London

33 Heller, H., 1950. *Experientia*, *6*, 368–75

34 Hench, P. S., Kendall, E. C., Slocumb, C. H. and Polley H. F., 1949. *Proc. Mayo Clin.*, *24*, 181–97

35 Houssay, B. A., 1959. In *Comparative Endocrinology*, proceedings of the Columbia University Symposium, 1958, ed. A. Gorbman, 639–67. New York

36 Houssay, B. A., Foglia, V. G., Smyth, F. S., Rietti, C. T. and Houssay, A. B., 1942. *J. exper. Med.*, *75*, 547–66

37 Hunter, J., 1837. *The works of John Hunter, with notes by J. F. Palmer*. London

38 Huxley, J. S., 1935. *Biol. Rev.*, *10*, 427–41

39 Knowles, F. G. W., 1963. *Proc. Roy. Soc. B.*, *141*, 248–67

40 Knowles, F. G. W. and Carlisle, D. B., 1956. *Biol. Rev.*, *31*, 396–473

41 Knowles, F. G. W., Carlisle, D. B. and Dupont-Raabe, M., 1955. *J. mar. biol. Ass. U.K.*, *34*, 611–35

42 Loewi, O., 1921. *Pflügers. Arch. ges. Physiol.*, *189*, 239–42

43 Marshall, A. J., 1961. *Biology and comparative physiology of birds*, vol. II. New York and London

44 Marshall, A. J., 1960. *Physiology of reproduction*, edited by A. S. Parkes, vol. 1, pt. 2 (chapter 11 by J. M. Dodd). London

45 Maynard, D. M., 1961. *Gen. comp. endocrinol.*, *1*, 237–63

46 Mering, J. von and Minkowski, O., 1889. *Naunyn-Schmiedeberg's Arch. exp. Path. Pharmak.*, *26*, 371–87

47 Miller, M. R. and Wurster, D. H., 1959. In *Comparative Endocrinology*, proceedings of the Columbia University Symposium, 1958, ed. A. Gorbman, 668-80. New York

48 Minkowski, O., 1893. *Naunyn-Schmiedeberg's Arch. exp. Path. Pharmak.*, *31*, 85–189

49 Munsick, R. A., Sawyer, W. H. and Van Dyke, H. B., 1960. *Endocrinology*, *66*, 860–71
Uranga, J. and Sawyer, W. H., 1960, *Amer. J. Physiol.*, *198*, 1287–90
Sawyer, W. H., Munsick, R. A. and Van Dyke, H. B., 1961. *Endocrinology*, *68*, 215–25

50 Neuman, W. F., 1960. 1st International Congress of Endocrinology, Copenhagen. Advance Abstracts of short communications, edited by Christian Hamburger. Acta endocr. (Kbh.), suppl. 50, 109–12

51 Oliver, G. and Schäfer, E. A., 1895. *J. Physiol., Lond.*, *18*, 230–76

52 Oliver, G. and Schäfer, E. A., 1895. *J. Physiol. Lond.*, *18*, 277–9

53 Rasmussen, H., 1960. 1st International Congress of Endocrinology, Copenhagen. Advance Abstracts of short communications, edited by Christian Hamburger. Acta endocr. (Kbh.) suppl. 50, 105–8

54 Ruysch, F., 1690. In *A short history of medicine*, 2nd ed., 1962, C. Singer and E. A. Underwood, 516. Oxford Univ. Press

55 Sanger, F., 1959. *Science*, *129*, 1340–5

56 Sawyer, W. H., Munsick, R. A. and Van Dyke, H. B., 1960. *Endocrinology*, *67*, 137–8

57 Selye, H., 1949. *Textbook of endocrinology*, 2nd ed. Acta Endocrinologica, Montreal

58 Simpson, S. A., Tait, J. F. and Bush, I. E., 1952. *Lancet*, *2*, 226–8

59 Starling, E. H., 1905. The Croonian Lectures, *Lancet, 2* 339–41, 423–5

60 Starling, E. H., 1914. *Proc. Roy. Soc. Med., 7,* pt 3, Therapeutic Sect. 29–31

61 Steiger, M. and Reichstein, T., 1937. *Nature, Lond., 139,* 925–6

62 Verney, E. B., 1926. *Proc. Roy. Soc. B., 99,* 487–517

63 Verney, E. B., 1947. *Proc. Roy. Soc. B., 135,* 25–106

64 Wells, M. J. and Wells, J., 1959. *J. exp. Biol., 36,* 1–33

65 Wigglesworth, V. B., 1954. *The physiology of insect metamorphosis.* Cambridge Univ. Press.

Index